MW01199412

KRESKIN
CONFIDENTIAL
The World's Greatest Mentalist Speaks Out

By

THE AMAZING KRESKIN

Inspiration for

The Great Buck Howard

authorHOUSE®

AuthorHouse™
1663 Liberty Drive
Bloomington, IN 47403
www.authorhouse.com
Phone: 1-800-839-8640

First published by AuthorHouse 3/27/2009

ISBN: 978-1-4389-7278-7 (e)
ISBN: 978-1-4389-7279-4 (sc)

Printed in the United States of America
Bloomington, Indiana

This book is printed on acid-free paper.

DEDICATION

To two dear and cherished friends.

To Lawrence Rose, who booked me at his home in Los Angeles for a private performance for his friends and business associates. He's become my attorney and counsel in all things showbiz. Because of his insight, experience and advice, he has made my excursion into the world of motion pictures remarkably rewarding and, at the same time, painless.

To Ric Meyers, an established author of great renown and my friend for many years I have special thanks. His understanding of my thinking enabled him to capture the hours of dictation I presented him with so he could edit and serve it to you in a manner that is digestible and clear.

1

AUTHOR'S NOTE

A few portions of my long out-of-print book *How to be (a fake) Kreskin* are incorporated in the following pages simply because I think they're just too juicy not to include.

Closing credit of the
Tom Hanks-produced movie
The Great Buck Howard:

Special thanks to
The Amazing Kreskin who has
entertained audiences for decades
and whose career inspired the character
of Buck Howard.

Like Buck, while many have tried,

no one has ever been

able to prove that

The Amazing Kreskin

uses any electronic devices

or hidden accomplices,

or that he is anything less than

100% truly amazing.

INTRODUCTION

To my way of thinking, there could not be a more appropriate time for this book to appear. After all, I've been urged to write, speak, and reflect upon what follows for years. But now with the plethora of "psychic programming" filling television and movie screens, the timing seems truly fortuitous. Just recently, there's been the unsuccessful, ill-fated, NBC series *Phenomenon*, followed by the capers of two refreshing characters called *Psyche*, then the very successful CBS series about a fake ghost whisperer turned police consultant named *The Mentalist*, then another series called *Lie to Me*, in which the investigator is supposed to be expert on detecting on whether suspects are telling the truth, and, finally, in culmination, to my personal pride and satisfaction, there's the Tom Hanks-produced movie *The Great Buck Howard* ... about a "questionably" legitimate mentalist.

So, it is long overdue that I reflect and expound upon the legitimate work of yours truly. Years ago, it was the prominent New York agent Howard Rapp who implored me to re-title my concerts and appearances with: "Will The Real Kreskin Please Stand Up?" With all the acts implying that they were reproducing what I do, and with all the self-styled mind readers who would appear (and then disappear) as fast as a rabbit in a top hat, he felt it was time that I share with my audiences a little bit of insight into what makes the "Real Kreskin."

By the way, this is not a book exposing stage illusions. I consider such actions reprehensible, and why would I do that? But I hope you'll find the following amusing, enlightening, and, at times, laugh-provoking (or is that laughable?) as I contrast my own work as a professional thought reader and entertainer with the performances around me, as well as recall and share fond memories of industry giants who have delighted and inspired me over the years.

⟾⟾◆⟽⟽

During the Vaudeville Era (which lasted from the late 1880's to the early 1930's) in much of the world, Houdini traveled with his escape act. Within a decade or so, there were escape acts all over the place purporting to imitate Houdini. Since, in those days, there was no radio, television, and very few silent movie theaters, many cities had up to eight Vaudeville houses, and, like twenty-four hour cable news networks today, those stages had to be filled or money would be lost. Sometimes, when a copy-cat escape act was across the street from Houdini, he would simply come into the rival theater, walk up on stage, explain in great detail what the person was doing, go into detail on how they were faking it, and then do an escape his way. This, invariably, "brought down the house" with ovations.

Ironically, from what I've been told by people who served as Houdini's assistants, as well as writer Walter Gibson (who created that legendary character *The Shadow*), Houdini was, at best, a second- (or even a third-) rate magician, who couldn't do the illusions competently at all. Even so, there's no doubt he was the world's greatest — and let me emphasize this — escape artist.

So, in the spirit of his tradition, I thought it would be refreshing for you, dear reader, to hear how what I've done has been copied, faked, or simulated through the years. As I said, no, this is not an expose of stage illusions, as I don't want to damage legitimate illusionists who spend years creating their work. But let's examine how the imitators of yours truly have borrowed from the fake mediums and other pseudo psychic purveyors and created the illusion of what I do.

I hope you'll get a kick out of this, and maybe, the next time you see one of these wannabees you'll imagine me striding into their TV shows or stage appearances, showing you how it's done, and, maybe, with your kind understanding and approval, bring down the house._

CHAPTER ONE
YOU'RE GETTING WARMER...!

In a by-gone era, the Vaudeville era (roughly 1880-1930), where entertainment was seen live, it was also not unusual for audiences to either form a rapport with, or be completely put off by, performers. Understand, too, that the Vaudeville theater owners knew that they were presenting entertainment for a family audience and literally could not afford to antagonize a substantial number of those attending.

Naturally, along came magic (and magicians) as one of Vaudeville's staple products. What would be more mystical than to see live magic taking place? It was its natural habitat ... not through something like a television set or movie screen. I hazard to say that magic is only truly magical when it is seen live and in person.

So, to satisfy its growing audience, new illusions were devised. The intrigue of sawing a lady in half has been seen in much of the modern world, and was done by hundreds upon hundreds of magicians. Along came what was hoped to be another milestone in magic: a giant, transparent glass case on stage, filled with water. And the magician would apparently walk across the water!

The illusion, no matter how ingenious, simply did not last. It offended too many people, as there was a taint of sacrilegiousness about it, since obviously it was too closely related to an important part of Christian scriptures. Vaudeville houses summarily banned the illusion.

In recent years, the illusion was going to be reattempted during a live performance in Canada and there was such a large protest against it that the act was cancelled. Not so on television. After all, television is only tuned into the feelings of its audience in retrospect. Rarely are viewers able to communicate an opinion immediately, even in live television, and even on cellphones.

The illusion of walking across water has been done at the edge of lakes and, yes, in swimming pools. To create credibility that there are not secret supports for the illusionist, individuals have appeared swimming in the pool and watching the magician walk literally within inches of them. The expression on the witnesses's faces are of remarkable astonishment.

Let's give those actors a round of applause for their fine, and at times, highly professional acting — for to be within a few feet of the stunt knowing full well how it is done, makes these performances all the more impressive. Heaven forefend that the viewer ever realized that these spectators were as phony as a three-dollar bill. They are not genuine spectators, but part of a larger deception. If the public realized that, they might feel betrayed — as certainly the illusion would not be part of a magician's art, but simple movie illusion.

Speaking of movies, I'm reminded of one of my favorite actors and his unique place in the history of stage magic. To this day I can't adjust to anyone else playing Inspector Clouseau except Peter Sellers. Bumbling yet subtle, I find myself almost laughing out loud when I think of certain scenes from the original *Pink Panther* in 1963 and its sequel, *A Shot in the Dark* (1964). But this man who could take on all kinds of characters played another role that very few know about.

There once was a psychic performer in England who was highly successful in his career, and deservedly so. But at an earlier time, he enacted a diabolical ruse on his unknowing Vaudeville audience. It was a change of pace for him. He didn't do an act like this before. In essence, he came on stage and was blindfolded, turning his back to the audience. So it really didn't matter if he was blindfolded, since his back was to the audience, and couldn't see them anyway.

Ironically, he could have been legitimately blindfolded, which is rare in the business, and very unusual for blindfold acts. He really could have been totally without sight, and it would have made no difference. Anyway, there he stood, and, one by one, people in the audience would stand up, holding an object, and, lo and behold, this great, psychically-gifted figure would announce aloud what they were holding, and in some detail.

They stood in different parts of the theater — some closer to the stage, others farther away. They could have, for all I know, been in the balcony, yet again and again he would announce what they were holding, even though he could not see (then again, he didn't have to see). The audience clearly heard him describing eloquent details of what was being held. He may have even given details about the kind of clothes the spectator in the audience was wearing. It was a great act, and the audience loved it. But as impressive as it was, this very fine performer could not carry this demonstration much further in his career. He couldn't really take it on tour — not that the theatre in which he performed was necessary for the stunt. He also couldn't take it into other countries, and, finally, he couldn't make it into a huge and successful career, even if he wanted to.

Because, you see, this gentleman had a friend who was also working to develop his skill in show business, and that friend was the aforementioned Peter Sellers. Oh yes, a young Peter Sellers, who, during this act, was propped up high in the flies of the stage, and was looking down at the audience with binoculars as each of the participants rose and held their object. And it was Peter Seller's voice that the audience heard. It was his voice, speaking through another microphone, imitating almost perfectly the voice of the performer on stage who everyone thought they were hearing. What a diabolical (and delightful) ruse! Thankfully Sellers had ambitions for better things, and ultimately became one of the great movie actors.

Make no mistake: I love movies. But I also love magic and I have found that rarely do the two mix well. Great magicians are really a live experience, and movie magic is a less connected experience — especially in this age of computer-generated images, where anything is possible (but increasingly uninvolving). I've often been asked where and when I fell in love with magic, movies, and the power of the human mind. In other words, what was the evolution that brought me to the point of appearing all over the world as The Amazing Kreskin.

Certainly I can remember the earliest "ah ha" moment in my life. Approaching the age of five, I was visiting relatives in Pennsylvania where I was given a comic book to occupy me. I started reading, and, well, fell in adolescent love. The comic book hero was most intriguing to my hungry brain. He was Mandrake the Magician, written and drawn by Lee Falk and Phil Davis. His comic demeanor just enchanted me, and, having started reading at an early age, I became embroiled in the aura of this wizard.

He really wasn't a magician who did magic tricks or slight of hand. Instead, he had hypnotic and, at times, telepathic abilities. He was able to solve crimes by mentally paralyzing criminals, or causing their guns to change to flowers or reptiles or what have you. This was all in the criminal's minds, of course.

Now, when other children were playing cowboys and Indians, yours truly was play-acting Mandrake the Magician with his friends, in a different sort of cops and robbers game. Mini-Mandrake (me) was fighting the friends who posed as crooks, and therefore, fighting crime.

But that all changed when I was around nine years old. It was raining one day, so we couldn't go out to play for the forty-three minute recess. Miss Curtis, our third grade teacher, decided to teach us a game instead. One of the students (I believe it was a Miss Jane Hamilton) left the classroom, while we all hid a beanbag somewhere in the class. Jane was called back and told to walk around, looking for the hidden object.

If she was far away from it, the rest of the class would say "colder," but if she approached it, they would say "warmer." If she got really close, they'd say "You're getting hot," and eventually she found the beanbag.

I was immensely disappointed, because I was never asked to play the game. There just wasn't enough time to get around to me. But when I left the classroom, I couldn't get the game out of my mind. Walking home for a mile or so (as I did for the thirteen years that I attended schools in my home town), I saw my brother. My mother was evidently out shopping, so we decided to go over to grandma and grandpa's house.

My grandfather was at work and my grandmother was attending to things. Both were from Sicily, and, although they didn't speak a word of English, we were extremely close to them. They rented the lower section of a two-family house that my grandfather and his construction friends had built by hand. In any case, I told my brother to go upstairs and hide a penny anywhere in the house. He called me when he was ready.

I walked upstairs. My grandmother was sitting behind a large kitchen table, obviously wondering what was going on. I wandered slowly towards my uncle's bedroom. He was at work. I walked into his room, climbed up on a maroon chair, and was able to reach behind a curtain rod … where I found the penny.

My brother knew something was special, because I never told him to tell me if I was getting hot or cold. He never spoke to me, but I had found the penny. My grandparents, being from Sicily, might have thought I had the evil eye, but the news of my accomplishment rapidly spread around the family, and I started performing at family affairs, Sunday get-togethers, what have you.

Then in fourth grade, Miss Galloway, my teacher, was intrigued when I started performing during show and tell. We did some magic tricks. I remember putting a glass of water on the table with a cloth under it, and pulling the cloth away without moving the glass or upsetting the water — a skill I'd seen in circuses.

A few days later, the Principal, Mr. Johnson, told me never to do it again. It turns out that my fellow classmates ended up breaking the dishware from their moms' kitchens trying to recreate the stunt. By then I was starting to introduce thought-reading experiments into class, and at one point I vividly remember bringing up someone's name. Gloria Palmer raised her hand, and I told her a movie she had seen a few days earlier. That moment stuck to me.

Miss Galloway was immensely impressed, and had me practice almost every Friday with my classmates. Two years later she reappeared as our teacher in sixth grade, so the classroom experiments continued. Those weeks were invaluable, as I not only learned about what I could do, but how the individuals in my classes reacted. Soon things I only instinctively guessed at became certainties. As a result, my thought-reading became more important, even though I was still doing magic.

In fact, classic magic was the majority of what I did, so by the time I was in junior high school I was performing for teachers and at private parties, among other things. After I had graduated to high school, I presented one of my first public concerts when I was in the ninth grade, and at about the age of fourteen. The high school auditorium was filled with schoolmates, friends, and family. I presented myself, as I had during assemblies, as "Kreskin," a mysterious Mandrakian performer and hypnotist (indeed, in articles around the country I was known as the youngest hypnotist in the United States).

During the performance, I had one teacher, Mrs. Long, thinking she was Liberace. But, by then, my thought-reading had become a more integral part of my program. As much as I loved magic, and performing magic, my thought-reading was taking on more and more time and substance during the show. What had all started with a game of "Hot and Cold" had developed into what many consider my most memorable contribution to the art of "mentalist entertainment."

But, just like me finding that hidden penny, I will secret more about my "hide and seek" adventures later in this book. For now, I'll hope you join me on a parallel journey into a world of legendary friends, as well as those who hoped to do what I do without putting in all the years of reading, studying, practicing, and honing that I have ... with pleasure.

CHAPTER TWO
THE GREAT ESCAPIST

One of Harry Houdini's most famous stunts was one he talked about many times throughout his career, and it has been recounted in many writings about his escape work. Indeed, it was an integral part of the plot in the 1953 movie *Houdini* starring Tony Curtis and Janet Leigh. Tony Curtis' performance as Houdini was colorful and refreshing, but vastly different from the real Houdini persona.

The stunt is the one in which Houdini was handcuffed in bitterly cold Detroit, and dropped through a hole in river ice. It was an extremely challenging and dangerous stunt. A normal, unathletic and untrained person, would be close to paralyzed by the cold within seconds, and die from hypothermia shortly after. Now add to that fact that Houdini was also incarcerated and restricted.

If you saw the movie, you'll know what happened. It's the same if you read some of the real-life reports of the incident. He ultimately escaped, but he misjudged what he was doing because there was water current, which moved Houdini away from the opening in the ice. I can just imagine what a terrifying experience that must have been. One could hardly wonder how much longer you could survive, if you had the wherewithal to even conceive such a rational thought under those circumstances.

You can't hold your breath very long under water even at the best of times, let alone handcuffed and in the freezing cold. Can you imagine the incredible panic that must have possessed him? But Houdini was a survivor, and had been from his youth as a Hungarian refugee. Somehow his well-honed instinct discovered that, between the sheet of ice over the water and the flowing water itself, there is a space. How in the world he did it writers can only speculate, but he was able to float under the ice with his nose above the water line until he found his way back and was able to pull himself up while being pulled out.

That was a gigantic stunt of almost unimaginable danger. Houdini recounted it many, many times. Only one problem. On the specific day of the stunt he often talked about, which was later carefully researched and studied, there was no ice. It was so warm on that day in Detroit that ice was not reported in any area of the city, let alone on a fast-moving river.

Houdini had successfully created another milestone in his legend with his eloquent story telling. Yours truly knows of no escape artist who ever tried to protect himself with the safety of the air space in an ice flow. God forbid they do, because anyone who would ever attempt such a feat is destined to deadly failure. But as author Stephen King has been quoted, "I don't write what happened, I write what should have happened." Or, as they said in the great 1962 film, *The Man Who Shot Liberty Valance* (among other places): "When the legend becomes fact, print the legend."

Houdini did a similar, so-called, psychic turn later in his career for a very specific reason. To put that into context, it's helpful to understand that for many years Houdini was strictly a Vaudeville act. Although there were times when Houdini's show lasted up to ninety minutes (when he was incarcerated in a cabinet and the audience sat there waiting, with tremendous anticipation, even apprehension, as the band played) he was usually only on stage for around twenty minutes.

He did a couple of escapes, and usually ended with an escape that was designed by someone in the town in which he was appearing. That person would come to challenge him during his performance — bringing in a special box, or lock, or having a especially constricting way of tying him. Sure, there were times when Houdini took his time to escape from an incarceration or a cabinet. Or, more likely, he had already escaped and was simply reading a magazine or a comic book while listening to the audience get more and more excited. When he found that the excitement had reached its peak, or was even starting to diminish, he would suddenly burst out, having miraculously escaped! Huzzahs ensued, faith was restored, and Houdini's fame was ensured.

But when Vaudeville passed from the scene, the twenty-minute act was passé, and Houdini decided to do a full-evening magic show. I mentioned earlier that this was not his strongest skill. Despite his renown, even his kindest critic couldn't help but notice his stiff stage presence in many silent films and non-escape performances. So, in this full evening show, he showed his true strength in the escape portion of his program. The magic part of the show was the weakest, but the most controversy was stirred by a third segment: where he sought to expose fake mediums.

Houdini was very close to his mother and after her passing, he didn't take kindly to people who said they could put her spirit in contact with him. He would publicly attack mediums, even in the town he was in. He knew they, or their confederates, were often in the audience, but there was one thing he didn't explain to his audience even though he was exposing fake psychics and mediums.

He would begin to tell them things about the people in the audience, and different people would stand and acknowledge the truth of what he was saying. He would relate a few details about their work, or where they lived, or some interesting tidbit of the day concerning people he had never met before … people he had never seen … just to show that he could do it as casually as the mediums. But, despite his condemnation of the "spirit guides," the audience was never let in on how Houdini did his own "psychic channeling."

The people who worked at the theaters in each of the towns he performed in were less than impressed with this skill, but unlike today, there was a code of silence amongst theater people. They weren't looking for their fifteen minutes of fame at the expense of someone else, so they never explained that Houdini had made agreements with the box office to check people who were coming in, to see if they could pick up tidbits about them before the show, which were then duly passed on to the legendary escape artist.

Don't get me wrong. There has never been an escape artist since the days of Houdini to compare with him. He truly was the greatest escape artist in modern history. But there is a problem regarding escapery, and with Houdini's cunning and, sometimes, ruthless brilliance, one wonders how he would have extracted success in this day and age. For it is extraordinarily difficult for any escape artist to build on any real fame today.

Certainly not even if that escape artist has a television series. Why? Because most television shows today are recorded so they can be played during primetime, and the evening is not always the best time to set up live television. Virtually all talk and variety shows (except *Saturday Night Live*) are pre-recorded. Today, a live show is a special occasion, not business as usual. Well, that pretty much destroys the impact of an escape artist. After all, escapery, unlike any other form of magic, rests largely on the danger factor. Most great escapes have a sense of criticalness to them — danger that could result in great physical harm and yes, even death.

That being the case, no matter how well-publicized an escape stunt is, anyone watching TV today is going to find it impossible to experience the impact that people felt watching Houdini back in the golden days of Vaudeville. More than likely, what with even home computers being able to generate broadcast-worthy special effects, audiences more often respond to these stunts with apathy, even boredom.

And, if the escapery that's being recorded doesn't succeed, or if the escape artist is hurt (or, God forbid, even killed), that piece of information will be on air, on line, and on web within seconds … pretty much ruining any effect before the taped show ever reached the air. Today, just having a show tells the fairly sophisticated viewer that whatever he or she is going to do is going to succeed, and they're going to escape successfully.

So the most important factor of anything involving the escape artists has been lost on television. Except on those rare occasions where programs have been live, it is impossible to create a sense of imminent danger or immediate suspense. And that's a truth even the great Houdini couldn't have escaped.

CHAPTER THREE

THE "MAGIC" OF TELEVISION

The weakening of magic on television ... no, the complete and actual breakdown of magic on television began a couple of decades ago. Understand, in the early days of television virtually all shows were live, not just *SNL*, news, and sports. *The Ed Sullivan Show*, which was obviously the most successful Vaudeville-esque variety-type show in U.S. history, was happening at the moment you were watching it. If an accident took place or someone fell on camera, it was not done over again — it was part of the show.

And when you saw a magician (and there were some great sleight of hand artists who appeared), you knew you were seeing the real thing. Since then, the integrity of magic has dismounted. When you saw the well-publicized illusion as gigantic as the Statue of Liberty being caused to vanish, something within you questioned what you were seeing. Well, at least I did. After all, if it were really happening, wouldn't people in New York and New Jersey look out the window and notice the Statue of Liberty was no longer there? It would have caused a crisis … or, at least, it would have caused tremendous word of mouth.

So it was the beginning of the age of illusion, making magic on television as "real" as "reality TV." Understand that, at an earlier time in television history, the networks would not have allowed such a falseness to take place. The people who ran the networks were European immigrants, and had a sense of theatrical history. They also had a certain sense of honesty with their audience and did not want to jeopardize that (outside of the great game show scandals of the 1950's, of course, immortalized in Robert Redford's film, *Quiz Show* in 1994).

When Arthur Godfrey did a magic show on his hour Wednesday night CBS-TV series, it wasn't the best, but even Walter Winchell pointed out it was honest and legitimate. In recent years, we see a lot of outdoor magic. We've even seen people floating between buildings, and cars vanishing at great speed. Of course, amongst those in the know, the question of trick photography is raised. People, even outside the intelligencia, are more sophisticated today.

There have been scenes where the magician is being put in a container, disappearing, and suddenly reappearing on the top of the building. To maintain credibility, crowds were gathered to watch the illusion. In the case of floating between buildings, the audience on the ground witnessed the illusion. I can't help but wonder, however, why there wasn't pandemonium from cars driving by, or from other people on the street. Surely, even in jaded Manhattan, seeing someone floating between buildings wouldn't even raise an innocent bystander's eyebrow?

What makes it difficult for me to accept the magic at home is when I realize that the people on the ground are actually seeing nothing. I repeat, nothing. They are acting and behaving as if they are seeing something, but they've been rehearsed over and over again. When you see that in a motion picture, you know it. From the early days of movies, when a magician appeared on the screen and made a person in a cabinet disappear, you knew that the person got out of the cabinet with editing, not actual stage magic. But when they create that magic nowadays on television, the person is put in the container with the crowd around them, the camera moves to the audience, and, meanwhile, the person simply gets out of the box and goes to the other area overhead.

There were some good thespians amongst that audience. They made a lot of people who believe these modern TV tricks are actually happening with skill and verve. But more than one magic-loving

Hollywood producer have told me that they feel this is betraying the public, for they're not really seeing a magic act.

So a magician walks into a shopping mall, goes up to an area where there's a window of some kind, covers it for a moment, and when he removes the cover there's a guy behind the glass, and the audience cheers. Give that audience credit! How well they cheered! Especially for something that is an absolute ruse. There was no theatrical magic. There was no stage illusion at all. The home audience is being betrayed.

Recently, another "magical" stunt was shown on television in which a car was to be run through a strong brick or concrete wall. The magician/driver was in real danger as the car sped toward the wall. Well, without going into too many details or mentioning the specific performer, the car hit the wall, crashed through, and the magician disappeared … of course to reappear elsewhere quite intact.

By now, loads of people (non-magicians, by the way) have seen the video of the stunt, but many might have missed a salient fact. When the car hit, it was not the same length of the car that was shown approaching the wall. Hmmm ... perhaps a current of air pressure diminished the length of the car ...?

There's a problem with all this, because it breaks down the honesty of a great illusion. I know that's a tricky idea, but it bears repeating. It breaks down the honesty of a great illusion. In other words, it betrays all the hard work behind the skill of a true professional magical artist. The magic you see live and in person is the result of years of great imagination and grand invention. It takes endless practice, exhaustive understanding of human nature, wit, verve, and even mathematical engineering. But that all becomes moot in the hands of TV short-cutters. They make it more difficult to trust a legitimate performer on television.

And the problem with magic is that unless you see it live, it loses some of its ... well ... magic.

Johnny Carson realized this and would never, to the day he died, allow something to be faked, or trick camera work to be used, to create illusion. Neither would Ed Sullivan. But sadly those gentlemen are gone. Whatever their faults, they would never be knowingly party to a betrayal of their audience. The basic problem with all this "fake reality" is that all magicians are diminished when that TV "magician" is unable to duplicate in person what he created through TV technology.

For instance, some years back a "prophet/fortuneteller/psychic" was certainly popular in the media not only because of her columns but because of her live appearances. She predicted the personal future of various celebrated individuals — including the prediction of John F. Kennedy's presidential election. Her name was Jean Dixon, and she was a rather colorful, amusing woman. Her apparently successful predictions of the presidency were a bit confusing because in an earlier Sunday supplement magazine piece, she had predicted that Nixon would win. So, consequently, her public utterance of one candidate winning and her previous interview saying that the other candidate would win left her in a win-win situation. As soon as the election was settled, she was quick to refer to the "correct prediction" … conveniently forgetting the other one.

More than a decade later, I met an individual who worked for a company involved in Dixon's columns and predictions. He revealed to me that she could often refer to her predictions coming true because, in some areas of the country, her predictions read one way, while in other areas, her predictions were just the opposite. Whatever happened, she would only refer to the newspapers in which her predictions corresponded.

Of course I have often wondered about self-styled psychics or fortune tellers. Specifically; why they don't spend more time at racetracks? One answer, which has been given by many professed psychics, is that they can't really make any predictions for themselves. It just doesn't work!

There was another psychic who wasn't terribly well-known outside the borders of tinseltown. She had one of her friends, who was evidently very close to Johnny Carson's *Tonight Show* bandleader Doc Severinsen. This particular psychic, after a tragic event took place in the United States, showed evidence that she had earlier predicted the incident on a local television show. She added to her credibility by insisting that doubters watch the videotape of her making the prediction. How could anybody quarrel with such evidence? Though the incident in question was a tragedy, it was one that a certain kind of personality would try to take advantage of, whether it be via tabloid media or what have you.

In this case, apparently to her credit, she had made the prediction and all could clearly see it was made on the tape of the show upon which she had appeared. Well, what can I say? Not much … except this. When you have even more than one person involved in a con, there is always a chance that the facts will leak out sooner or later. Oh, yes, she did make the prediction and yes, what she said in the prediction on the video was exactly correct. The problem was the time frame. She had gone back to the studio long after the event took place, gathered the crew together, and convinced them to record her prediction. Her claim to fame was much shorter than expected, and it is no surprise she is forgotten.

When the final story broke, I was relieved that it didn't tarnish Severinsen's reputation or his relationship with Carson and the *Tonight Show*. There is little to be said for "guilt by association."

———◆———

Here's another one of my favorite examples, from this past year while I was performing in Indianapolis, Indiana. I was approached by a professional investigator who asked me if I was aware of what non-disclosure clauses were. With some slight sense of reluctance, I stated I was. Turns out he thought it would be interesting for me to note that government and non-government investigators were learning that more and more participants on "reality shows," in which people were supposed to be responding "spontaneously," were indeed far from such — and to prevent disclosure on their part were not only made to sign non-disclosure agreements.

There are even specific cases that I became aware of where participants were threatened with possible major lawsuits if they wrote or were interviewed about the behind-the-scenes shenanigans. It's becoming more and more obvious to even the biggest fans of these shows that the "unscripted" have scriptwriters and the "undirected" have directors just off camera.

The result is that it's difficult to believe anything that's happening in reality shows is actually real. That's harmful to "unscripted" shows, but it's fatal to the TV magician or escapist.

⟫◆⟪

Some seasons ago NBC introduced a new primetime series called *Phenomenon*, in which performers apparently from different parts of the globe demonstrated their "paranormal" abilities and vied to win an essentially meaningless prize. It had a strange marriage of hosts. First, there was one Uri Geller, a psychic who, in the distant past, created a reputation for bending metal with just his mind. Next, there was illusionist Criss Angel.

Actually, to say this was a strange marriage is putting it mildly. Angel would frequently challenge Geller about his psychic abilities in a demeaning way. Apparently, this was supposed to make "good television," but if you look at the tapes, you may conclude that Geller was the winner. Whether you believe his bending metal shenanigans, he handled himself with remarkable grace and displayed a quality of showmanship in just letting the barbs roll off him like water off a duck's back.

It was obvious that Angel was trying to do a Houdini, or at least reflect the great escape artist's attack of spirit mediums. One hopes that he was not modeling himself after Houdini, for, as the late Walter Gibson (who was very close to Houdini, and an authority on magic and the paranormal) often told me, "Houdini was, in many cases, far more dishonest than the mediums he was attacking."

I have a full twenty-four hours of interviews with Gibson that reveal a side of Houdini nobody has ever written about ... but that's another story.

It's little wonder that *Phenomenon* was so unsuccessful. Certainly it didn't add to Geller's credibility, even though we are led to believe that it was Geller's idea, and he's carried it to other countries to produce a similar series. Performers on the show were bending metal more dramatically than I remember Geller doing. Indeed, it was unimpressive to see a person on the show doing the same thing that Geller had claimed to have been done by some psycho-kinetic mind power years before.

Let's examine psycho-kinetic powers. I've never claimed to have any. My abilities are those of perceiving and influencing people's thoughts, both mentally and through suggestion. But we're told that the psycho-kinetic abilities are sometimes so spontaneous, as Geller used to say, that metal would sometimes spontaneously bend around him without any conscious effort.

That being the case, I can see certain dangers. Would you want such a person with such gigantic, remarkable mind powers to be next to you in a car or plane? Would you want such a person near an individual with a pacemaker? I would say hell no. Keep them miles away from me. But somehow I don't think any of us need to worry.

Naturally, as time went on, it began clear that *Phenomenon* was all a TV trick. Word had leaked out about how theatricality was used to attempt making the show more appealing, and how some of the performers' stunts were being further enhanced by camera work, editing, etc. It wasn't one of my greatest accomplishments to predict exactly which performer would win, and that the series would not be renewed.

How did I predict who would win? Not because of the performers' talent. I've seen many others who are equally talented. It was because I knew where the contestants had performed before. If anyone had checked the database of colleges a competitor had appeared at, it was natural to assume that the contender had invited his audiences to vote for him. *Phenomenon*, as a result, was far less phenomenal.

Understand that when I made my two predictions about *Phenomenon*, the rumor got around that I had proved the show as rigged. I did not, and had no intention of doing so. Was it rigged? Sure, the stunts were rigged. There were three major problems. Two of them were the hosts. The third was the clear, obvious, design of the systematic structure for each of the psychics, giving me the feeling that, more than anything else, I was watching a magic show, and that's exactly what it was.

⟫◆⟪

Television has truly increased the popularity of poker. Now, with a number of channels, both cable and network, covering poker games, the interest has extended to all ages. It's not unusual anymore for me to find college students passionately involved in this game of skill and chance. What is worrisome is to see some of these same students going to the ATMs in gambling casinos to fulfill their gambling habit.

There have been a number of motion pictures through the years that have embraced poker's psychological intrigue. I think *The Cincinnati Kid* (1965) is one of the most compelling films ever centered around the game of poker. If you want to see classic portrayal, observe the brilliant acting of the late Edward G. Robinson, playing almost a guru of the game.

Me? I cannot play poker anywhere in the civilized world. Well, of course I could, but I don't. I don't know about the uncivilized world, but I doubt if I would leave in one piece. Come to think of it, that would probably also be true if I tried to play poker in the civilized world. Now that I consider it, would Vegas or Atlantic City be considered the civilized or uncivilized world?

No matter. One of my closest, dearest, friends, the late Dr. Sy Fish — a fine dentist on the east coast who I thought was a brilliant poker player — used to remind me that I could clean up if I played. The problem is how the other players would take my involvement. There they'd be: concentrating on their cards and thinking of the plays they could make, while I'm sitting across from them, reading their thoughts. I might win, but I don't think I'd last long.

Now, blackjack is a different story. There are many casinos that will permit me to play, because there are no cards that anyone's focusing on. The dealer doesn't know the next card coming up, and there are a lot more cards involved. So, there, my advantage is in how I handle the game, not in judging or perceiving cards that other people are concealing.

Many casinos now deal from a "shoe" that contains six to eight card decks to discourage, or make it almost impossible, to count cards. But here's a tip. The counting of cards is not really the greatest advantage in the game. A deck of cards has a memory.

As certain cards are dealt from the deck, there is an advantage to the player, and, in many other cases, an advantage to the house.

Obviously, if an awful lot of tens or aces are depleted from the deck, the player has less percentage of drawing a twenty (that is, two tens, or blackjack, an ace and a ten, etc). Common sense should tell you that. If fives and sixes pour out of the deck, the dealer has less cards to make twenty-one (or less than twenty-one without breaking or busting, i.e., going over 21, and therefore losing).

You see, a player has a chance when playing blackjack, because the deck will sometimes swing in the favor of the player and other times swing in favor of the house. That's what I mean when I say the deck has a memory. Incidentally, I hear of casinos that deal out of a shoe that shuffles every hand. Those cards are drawn from a deck, but are immediately put back into a shuffling machine that makes the next hand brand new.   Anybody who plays that game is a sucker at best, and a fool at worst. I can't imagine the house attempting to attract people using such a ruse. Certainly no one in charge would feel it would be fair to the average person. But, just so you know, there are places that shuffle the deck every hand, as much as an abomination as that is.

So naturally, when magicians have been shown on television going to a casino and winning, understand those games, and scenes, are rigged. The magician is not suddenly having a lucky streak. You are not seeing the art of magic. You're seeing the art of theatrical movie making — creating the deceptive illusion that the performer has legitimately won large amounts of money.

By the way, if you're playing against an eight-deck shoe, you will not often win three or four hands in a row. In an eight-deck shoe, because there are so many small cards, the dealer rarely breaks … maybe one out of eight times. That's the mathematical fact of things — one out of eight times. In most cases, if you have been going through such a shoe, there's only eight or nine minutes of winning time, on average, in one hour of playing. If you like those odds, more power to you. But to me … well, let's just say it's not the best thing that ever happened to the game of blackjack.

A few years ago I set something of a record and received international press coverage. All I did was walk into Resorts in Atlantic City late one night after performing my show. Well, to be honest, that wasn't all I did. I sat down to play blackjack, starting with just two hundred dollars. In a few hands I was down to about twenty dollars, so I went to a fifteen-dollar table.

My road manager and I had a long trip back home, so I decided to play it out. Forty minutes later the table was surrounded by scores of people, even though it was the middle of the night. The nearby slot machines area had grown unusually quiet after I won twenty-two hands in a row. That broke a record from a few years earlier when someone won eighteen hands in a row. Then again, that was also me.

My most dramatic blackjack game, however, was in Aruba some years ago. After finishing my show on closing night after a two-week appearance, I went to the casino to play blackjack. I sat down with about thirty dollars. To the excitement of my road manager and the chagrin of the dealer (as well as the casino), I kept winning. It was most evident they were hoping I would lose my money back to them, so they kept the casino open after the closing hour … with me as the only player.

Eventually I went back to my hotel room to deal with the most difficult packing job I have had in years. Believe me, packing more than twenty-two thousand dollars along with my clothes is not that easy.

Bear in mind, however, that while gambling magic shows are all "edited for television," and there are myriad stories of winning games of chance, remember what happened to *The Cincinnati Kid*. The truth of the matter is that casinos are not funded by winners.

CHAPTER FOUR

ABOVE PAAR

I never knew the late Jack Paar, but as a college student I sat, transfixed, watching this man for an hour and forty-five minutes each night on NBC's *The Tonight Show* from 1957 to 1962 — pouring out his troubles, complaining about behind-the-scene incidents, admonishing some of the people he worked with or stars who wouldn't appear on his show, and even debunking the gossip columnists of his day (weakening their hold on a gullible public). He had succeeded in doing this, along with Merv Griffin and a few other small screen interviewers, because celebrities had discovered something special about that era's talk shows.

If you went on the air and talked about your scandal, or quasi-scandal, and explained it or expounded upon it, that took the heat out of the columnists' breaking the story. The columnists no longer had an exclusive, and very often would have to report about it after the fact. The celebrity also found an opportunity to respond to the columnists, and Paar did that eloquently—talking back to people like the then-powerful Walter Winchell, who did not have as great a public platform as Paar.

Winchell had an extraordinarily successful daily gossip column — certainly one of the most powerful columns in the western world, but, even then, newspapers were falling into the shadow of television. Paar even reached a point where he challenged Winchell to come on the show with him, and, of course, Winchell was a no-show. He knew from long experienced that it's hard to beat a person at their own game ... and, perhaps more importantly, in their own setting.

Jack was also intrigued by magic, although he wasn't very good at it. He did some trivial things, but every once in a while he'd come on stage with a turban or something similar, and proceed to do a psychic act. Someone in the audience would stand, he'd ask them their name, and then he would tell them what city they lived in, part of their phone number, or what have you. And while no one really believed that he was telepathic, he presented it in an amusing and intriguing manner.

It wasn't a new act. He borrowed it from some comedy Vaudeville acts, or minstrel shows that were put on by Kiwanis, Rotary, or other clubs in the states and other parts of the world. There were always live, fund-raising, shows in various towns where amateur thespians put on various variety turns. Usually, however, there was a humorous exposure at the end of the psychic act. Jackie Gleason and Art Carney even did a take-off of one on an episode of the perennially popular, pioneering sitcom *The Honeymooners*.

Jack Paar, however, held his big reveal in reserve. Finally, however, he relented, and in *TV Guide*, which, at that time, was the most popular television magazine in America, Paar revealed what was going on through a series of pictures. As I said, he borrowed from the live shows done around the country. Sometimes in these shows the medium sat at a table and had people in the audience call out a name, after which he would announce their telephone number or the like. Then, at the end of the routine, the tablecloth would slowly fall, revealing someone under the table looking up each name in the phonebook, and passing the info to the sham swami. The audience roared.

Paar sophisticated it. The reason he was wearing a turban was because he had earphones, and some member of the show would simply radio the information to him. Easy as that.

But as much as I admired Jack Paar, I have to admit I was more inspired by one of his successors. Through the years, my experiences with Johnny Carson have been related time and time again. After

Johnny's retirement from *The Tonight Show* in 1992 after thirty years, I became even closer to Fred de Cordova, who first directed the show, then became producer, and, ultimately, executive producer. We reflected on the changes that had taken place, even in guests on talk shows, including how the concern for their audiences had changed.

Fred would see the difference in their showmanship, training, and grandeur. He was not living in the past, but he had lived through a show where there were remarkable standards. People were not just brought on because they'd been sleeping with a public figure, but because of their talent, and their ability to communicate with their audiences.

It is not well known, but my first appearance with Carson was not on *The Tonight Show*. I wasn't even known outside of a few northeastern states at that time. Before Johnny ever went on national TV, he was hosting a daily half-hour game show in New York called *Who Do You Trust*. The announcer was Ed McMahon.

The format was similar to the far more successful and long-running *You Bet Your Life* starring Groucho Marx. On both shows, people were brought in to be interviewed before being asked quiz questions worth a small amount of money. The entertainment value came from the wit and wisdom of the host.

Yours truly appeared on the program with a very important companion … my mother. I was in college, and, again, not very well known. I did not win a lot of money. In fact, it was one of the less comfortable shows I had done, since I was not used to national television, let alone the quiz show setting. But Carson was kind, and Ed McMahon was quite generous with his concern for the well-being and comfort of my mother.

Some years later, Steve Allen left *The Tonight Show* in New York and moved out to California to create the one-hour, late night *Steve Allen Show*. Both shows became extremely popular with high school and college students. I stayed up late each night to watch, because, to my way of thinking, Steve Allen was the greatest wit that I'd ever seen.

His producers heard about me, and flew me out to Los Angeles. There was no rehearsal, because I couldn't rehearse. Even then I had standards, and the last thing I would ever do was run through what I was planning. It had to be spontaneous, since I was going to be reading the thoughts of members of the audience and Steve Allen's cast.

Well, Steve introduced me with a very nice intro. He said they were all interested in extra sensory perception and telepathic phenomena, among other things. The curtain opened and I walked out. Well, in those days television lights were blinding … literally blinding. So, instead of gracefully reaching over and shaking hands, I tripped and practically fell flat on my face.

It got a quiet chuckle. Steve was very nice about it and didn't make an issue, although he could have since he was a fast-thinking ad-libber. Johnny Carson had seen the incident and created Carnac the Magnificent, who always tripped on the way to the desk. As I said to Johnny on one of my last appearances with him, "You never let me forget my first national appearance on television toppling over on the Steve Allen Show!"

And Johnny said, "Oh, the Great Carnac." By the by, Carnac's dialog came from Steve Allen (as Jane Meadows, Steve Allen's wife, always reminded me). Steve did a routine in which he was a brash, outrageous newspaperman who'd tell a story, and then announce the headline, which was always a funny take-off on the story itself. That comedic format came from Vaudeville. And since Steve Allen's mother had been a famous vaudevillian known as Belle Montrose, the idea of telling a funny question after mentioning a leading answer was natural for him.

Only those who know me closely have any idea how far I've stuck my neck out in some of my appearances on television. Talk about spontaneity. Every time I did the Carson show, I never went through a rehearsal. I would simply tell them what I planned to do. Carson had a crackerjack camera team. They could catch something as it fell off the table — as happened a couple of times in my appearances sitting next to Johnny.

But in one case I planned a very dramatic test using Johnny as a subject. Very few people realize that the day before the show, I received a call from NBC. I did not know the caller, but they found out what I was going to do and suggested I do not do it. Of course I agreed to that. I didn't want to jeopardize my future with the show. But it surprised me it came from a person whose name I didn't recognize.

A few hours later I received a call from Johnny Carson's secretary. I had a very good rapport with her, and from time to time she'd give me a call (I suspect, on occasion, unbeknownst to Johnny ... just to appraise me of something she thought I'd be interested in). Some of his other staff did the same thing, but that day it was her. She said I was going to get a call from Johnny. Would I be available? Of course I would be available.

He called me. I had never spoke to him on the phone. And he asked if I was approached about what I was planning to do tomorrow. Now this was New York City, and the show was to be filmed live. I said yes, I was told not to do it. He uttered a few colorful words, after which he said, "We are going to do it."

The next day I headed for the city. This was the one time I needed to see Johnny before the show. Not to cheat the audience, but to make sure he was capable of responding, and turmoil ensued. Being me, I missed the time set aside for me to meet with him. I finally got to the show only forty minutes before the live telecast. I was extremely upset with myself. I just do not function this way, and I was very apprehensive.

I talked to the staff. They told me that Johnny said "no problem." He knows he can do it, and he'll go through with it. I said to the staff, "No no, that's not the whole picture. I need to see him to lock his thinking." They didn't understand what I meant. I said, "Please, if I don't see him before the show, I can't do the test."

It was a scenario that's deeply embedded in my mind. As Johnny's liaison walked me through the NBC hallways, she said, "You know, Kreskin, people don't meet Johnny before the show. It's very rare, especially this closely before show time." We arrived and there sat Johnny. It was a scene out of a crime movie. Johnny sat at a desk. The rest of the room was dark. He had papers in front of him. I realize, in retrospect, that it must have been his monologue. There was a lamp with a bare bulb, and he was just staring down at the table. You could hardly see his face. I learned that he considered his monologue the special moment of each night's show, so he poured his soul into it.

I said to him, "John, I know you're busy, but let me talk to you. This is the way I want you to think when I'm working with you. This is the way I want you to focus your thinking, your concentration. Trust me." He said, "I've got it, Kreskin."

That night was one of the wildest moments of my career. We talked about hypnosis. I said there was really no trance, no altered state. Through pure suggestion I could influence people. In hypnotic situations the only thing that was happening was suggestion. There was no altered state of consciousness. Then I said, "Johnny, I have something I'm going to do with you."

We walked over to the center of the stage. Ed McMahon and bandleader Doc Severinsen joined us, obviously wondering what was going on. I had Johnny close his eyes. I started counting, and somewhere between thirty seconds and a minute later, Johnny swayed backwards.

Ed, Doc and I caught him, then stretched him between two chairs — putting his head and shoulders on one, and his feet on the other. We stepped away. He was suspended.

This became a centerfold of *Parade Magazine,* a national Sunday newspaper supplement all over the United States. Well, there was one more part of the picture. There was another guest on the show, who had come out before me. I asked her to come over. She did, but was highly nervous, and, as I reminisced with her at a dinner a year ago, I had her sit on Johnny Carson's stomach.

That's right, on his middle, with her feet lifted off the floor. There was no illusion, no trickery, no magic. Through suggestion I had locked his muscles, and he really had no fear of the whole experience. When it was over, we lifted her off, stood him up, and all was well.

Johnny told me during the commercial break that it almost seemed like a light-weight baby was sitting there, not the full-grown Bette Midler, who, at that point, wondered if she would ever be invited to the show again since she had sat on one of the NBC's top stars.

Of course she did. In fact, she was honored as his very last guest on his very last show, singing him an unforgettable rendition of "One More for my Baby and One More for the Road."

<hr />

In 2007 we lost a fabulous radio and television broadcaster by the name of Tom Snyder. I knew him very well, having worked with him many times through the years. Most people remember him for going on the air after *The Tonight Show* with a one-hour interview program called *Tomorrow* in the days before Conan O'Brien or Jimmy Fallon. It was so well done that it lasted from 1973 to 1982.

Tom Snyder was an inquisitive, opinionated, but learned man who could interview almost anyone. I first got to know him during the early days of my own career. Back then, he was broadcasting a show out of KYW in Philadelphia. In the latter days of his show, he had up to three guests, and I often appeared with him. But in the earlier days, he had an hour morning show, complete with studio audience, that spotlighted a single guest, and that program was even a greater pleasure for me.

Sooner or later, he would have me attempt some thought-reading experiments or effects with the audience. Incidentally, one of the first times I did the show, it turned out to be a remarkably traumatic experience, unbeknownst to him or his staff. I was driving from eastern Pennsylvania to Philadelphia — not that long a trip. I'd been staying at a dear friend's place, who is a highly respected physician.

The problem was that my judgment of distance and time on a business day was not spot-on, as I had never driven to Philadelphia on a weekday morning before, and panic ensued. Sound familiar? I arrived at the station after Tom Snyder had gone on the air. I didn't know where to park, so I parked in front of the studio, jumped out of the car, and ran into the downstairs area.

Another popular talk show of the time, *The Mike Douglas Show*, also emanated from the KYW building. That one I knew well, having down more than a hundred appearances with him, but Tom Snyder's show was upstairs from that. I bolted up the stairs, only to discover that Tom was rerunning a clip from an earlier show that I did with him to vamp for time.

Happily, everything went well, and we were delighted with the results. I, especially, was relieved that I did not let him down. I stayed only a few minutes after the hour, as I had work elsewhere in the Pennsylvania area, and walked out of the studio with relief. Suddenly, a feeling of terror filled me. Oh yes, the great mentalist finally remembered that not only had I not known where to park, but I had double-parked on a main street in Philadelphia, and left the car running.

Now, over one hour later, I didn't know what to expect. I bolted out the door, and stood, surprised, to see my car still there, still running, doors unlocked. It hadn't been towed. It hadn't been ticketed. And when I jumped in that car and drove away, I was filled with one hell of a feeling of relief. Sometimes even I marvel at my own luck.

In any case, Tom Snyder and I had built a bond of trust. He often brought me on to discuss unexplained phenomena or strange theories of the mind, and we would often spend half-an-hour on the show, just the two of us. One day his producer told me that a self-proclaimed mentalist had managed to be booked on the show. This person said he had abilities in perceiving thoughts, and he referred to me frequently, so Tom good-naturedly had him on. After the person made his claims and comments, he decided to show Tom his abilities.

There were five objects put on the table in front of him. He told Tom, "I'll turn my head, and you touch one of the items. Don't pick it up, just touch it, and when you take your hand away, let me know, so I can turn around." Snyder went through with the instructions. The "mental wonder" moved his hand back and forth over the five items, and finally picked up one of them. It was the item that Tom had chosen, as all the viewers in the studio audience saw.

I believe he did this a second time … I think at Tom's urging. He turned around again, and lo and behold, picked the same object … but by then a light bulb had gone off in Tom's mind. To be more accurate, he smelled a rat. Ever a consummate host, Tom was always aware of his audience who sat close by. And when the "swami" did the stunt again, Tom noticed that a gentleman standing at the rear of the studio rubbed his eye.

Snyder checked with his producer. The eye-rubber had accompanied the performer. It became clear that, depending on which item Tom touched this individual in the back of the theater would signal the swami with a prearranged code: left eye, right eye, arms crossed, whatever. Tom was too much of a gentleman to openly expose him, but he said, "Why don't we do it differently this time? Instead of my touching the object, why don't I think of the item?"

For some miraculous reason, the performer was not able to do the test a third time. Tom thanked him for appearing on the show and let him leave. Apparently he was supposed to be on for a segment or two. I only know that it turned out to be a much shorter amount of time than the person, or Tom, had intended.

By the way, in recent years, this stunt has been updated. On a cable show seen five nights a week, on a couple of occasions, a magician showed an intriguing stunt. Wouldn't you know? He had five items on a table. He was sitting next to the host. He turned his face from the host, further exaggerating his inability to see by holding his hand over his face. He then told the host to pick up one of the objects. When the object was put back, he turned around and successfully found the object. Isn't that astonishing?

Today, the sophistication of this stunt has moved one giant step, especially in this electronic age. All the performer had to do was to have a secret assistant, but not the same as the one who sat in Tom Snyder's audience thirty years ago. The stooge or confederate could even be in the lobby, in the green room, or even backstage … as long as he could see a monitor. All the mental wizard needed was an electronic device that gave off either a slight current, and when the performer slowly moved his hand over the items, his buddy simply signaled by pressing his remote transmitter.

Let's take the stunt up one gigantic level: where the performer decides to risk a tremendous amount of money … let's say twenty million dollars, and has the money put in the trunk of a car outside of a hotel. Then the performer, who's been carefully guarded to prevent his knowledge of the right car, steps out of the hotel, walks to the cars, picks one, opens the trunk, and abracadabra, there's the money.

Do you think that such a performer would really risk such an amount of money, even if it was supplied by the network or hotel? Hell, no. Retrace the scenario. How would you do it? If you've been reading carefully, the answer would simply be the infamous electronic device.

Oh the performer might point to his ears and say, "I'm using no special electronics." Maybe not a hearing aid, or even a cellphone, but that doesn't mean that he doesn't have any other kind of vibrating mechanism ... which could increase as the magician walks closer to the car, and lessen if he walks away.

But what if his confederate isn't even among the specially selected crowd witnessing the event? Remember, this was at a hotel where a person sitting by any number of windows on either side of the street can see everything that's taking place. All the stooge has to do once the magician starts to search is to start signaling to bring the person closer to the item.

This sort of thing is truly below Paar ... or Allen, or Carson, or Snyder, or anyone in the medium who truly respects their audience.

CHAPTER FIVE

ALL'S WELL THAT ENDS WELLES

Orson Welles was a giant in show business history. His career covered so many mediums (if you'll excuse the expression): television, the legitimate stage, certainly motion pictures, and incidentally, early radio. Since we're talking about the mystic arts, Welles helped introduce a successful radio series based on the pulp magazine mainstay *The Shadow*. Created by Walter Gibson, a dear friend of mine whom I knew very closely for many years, he, like his creation, was an authority on many, many things. Certainly Walter knew all the great magicians. He even wrote for them.

He was also an authority on the paranormal — both the legitimate and fraudulent — and as an expert on magic and the trickery of fake mediums, he clearly believed in certain forms of paranormal phenomenon. In addition, he was an authority on crime. He would have to be, as he was one of the most prolific writers who ever lived, having authored more than three hundred novels. Although several Shadow movies have been made (with one being produced even as we speak), the cinematic versions have never gotten close to the literary effect.

In Gibson's books, (some still in print after eighty years), The Shadow was a rather questionable character — in that his ethics may have been closer to the criminal than to the police. Although he fought crime, he hid in the shadows to pursue his criminal with a remorseless, unsympathetic conviction that would be considered out of place in any court of law.

Along came radio, and it became clear that some technique needed to be used to capture the intrigue of the audience beyond the visual idea of The Shadow hiding in corners … and the angle was brilliant. In the introduction to each half-hour Shadow radio play (one of the most successful mystery shows ever in the history of radio), you hear a voice intone: "The Shadow has learned a strange hypnotic power to cloud men's minds so they can not see him…!" Then, as you hear the mystery unfold, somewhere usually late in the game, a criminal who thought he was getting away with murder would hear a strange, mocking, laugh. It was The Shadow, whom he couldn't see, because of an unusually special and powerful form of hypnosis.

That power to "cloud men's minds" became his special way of fighting crime. Orson Welles, with his remarkable voice, played one of the first radio Shadows, as well as his alter ego, Lamont Cranston. And although several other actors came before him, he set the standard to which other Shadow performers aspired. Although the hero lived on radio for more than twenty years, it was Welles' reading of the character's oft-quoted tagline that is best remembered. "Who knows what evil lurks in the hearts of men? The Shadow knows…!"

As great as he was, Welles had one problem with The Shadow. Very often, before they went on the air, someone else had to do the unique Shadow laugh so Welles could lock it into his mind. Welles was like many highly talented, very busy, radio actors. He'd often show up without having seen the script. As it was handed to him, he asked what kind of person he was playing, and then go on "cold," and live, dramatizing a script he had never read before. Such were the adventures of radio.

Off stage, Welles had an interest in magic, the occult, and mysticism. He would have loved to have been a great magician. Some people felt he thought he was. He wasn't. He tended to fumble a lot, using his dulcet voice and abundant charisma to cover for what he lacked in dexterity. He admired David Bamberg, who, in the role of the fictional character Fu Manchu, performed on stage throughout South

America, with raging success. Certainly Bamberg is one of the greatest illusionists of all times, and is part of a family dynasty.

If you saw Welles on television, sometimes performing illusions on *The Tonight Show starring Johnny Carson* or on some TV special, he really wasn't doing most of the work. In many cases his assistants were professional magicians themselves. His achieving magnificent magician status never came to pass, (thank heaven). But I will tell you what Welles told me the first time I met him — which is while I was performing at The New London Theater in London, England.

Welles was living in London at that time. I had the afternoon free, and met a friend of mine, Irv Tannen, who sold equipment to magicians and was a remarkable authority on magic as well as the deceptions of professional gamblers. We went out to eat and Irv spotted Orson sitting at the other end of the restaurant by himself. Irv went over, said hello to Welles, whom he had known for years, and then came back to the table. He explained to me that Welles was a fan of mine, had admired me greatly through the years, and was going to join us.

We discussed great magicians, the not-so-great Houdini, and others who Welles didn't seem to think much of. He then started to explain an idea he had for a television show, and I got very uncomfortable. Irv saw that I just didn't feel right about it. Suffice to say that it rubbed me the wrong way and it probably wouldn't be helpful to go into detail just yet. Let's leave that dinner in the shadows, as it were, and move forward a number of years.

Welles would often appear on talk shows and do some kind of stunt, and, as often as not, the stunt backfired. For whatever reason, it just didn't work out, but he'd laugh it off and fun was had by all. Then he'd call Irv the next day and say, "Irv, what'd you think of me last night," and Irv would say "That was a piece of s@#!" Irv was very blunt, and Welles would simply say, "Yea, it was pretty bad, wasn't it?"

Irv was, apparently, one of the few persons Orson would listen to.

Once, on Dick Cavett's late night talk show, Welles said he was going to do a telepathic test. They picked a woman from the audience, handed her a deck of cards, and told her to leave the theater, go into the lobby, pick a card, and come back with the card hidden. Meanwhile, Welles had taken a card from another deck, and it was lying in front of him. He asked the woman if she had the card, and she said no. She started looking through the deck, and he got annoyed. Knowing him as I do, he was more than likely furious.

He said, "You go out and do it right," or something to that effect. Fortunately for anyone near Welles for the next few hours, she listened to him, because when she finally showed the card from the deck, he had picked the same card. The reason he was upset and almost blew the stunt is because, when she left, she didn't really pay attention. It turns out that, in the deck of cards, the first card had a note written on it instructing her to pick up one certain card in the deck, and to make sure she had that card chosen. She hadn't paid attention, so using her as a stooge didn't work the first time around.

Now let's fast forward once again. There is a book entitled *Backstage at The Tonight Show from Carson to Leno*, written by Don Sweeney, who was a musician from the east coast and had always wanted to work with Carson. Eventually Sweeney drove his car out to California to make his dream come true, but how do you get a job when you didn't know anyone connected to the show and didn't have any Burbank contacts?

Sweeney's solution? During the day he would go to NBC and take the guided tours. They don't seem to exist anymore — or if they do, they're cut back, which is a shame — but back in the 1970's, tourists would be guided around studios when shows usually were not on air. If you were lucky, you might see a rehearsal. Day after day Sweeney would attend these guided tours, and somehow find a way of ending up in the men's room, where, believe it or not, he incarcerated himself for God knows how many hours. By late in the afternoon, the audience was let into where *The Tonight Show* was filmed. I should know the studio's number, having done eighty-eight Carson shows, but being me, I don't. But Sweeney would lurk about, and, if he spotted an empty seat he would make a beeline for it.

But I digress. Even so, I enjoyed it so much I'll do it again. A couple of years ago, I was told there was a whole segment with me on *Entertainment Tonight* — the self-proclaimed "most watched entertainment news program in the world." I was surprised, since I didn't see myself on the show the night that I was told I appeared. It turns out that Sweeney was on the episode, saying that he was in the audience on one of the evenings when I was on *The Tonight Show*. As was typical, Johnny mentioned that I hadn't rigged anything, that I did not use confederates, and that I was doing my effect legitimately.

He turned to me and said, "Do you want me to pick five people in the audience?" I said, "Yes, Johnny." Can you believe that one of the people he picked was this gentleman who had envisioned working for Carson for so long? Sweeney went on to explain that the five volunteers, none of whom knew each other, were involved in a mental test I was doing. No trickery involved. He didn't speak as well of Welles and his stunts on the show ... as you will soon read.

Oh, by the way, a few days later this gentleman got a job on the show. He became one of bandleader Doc Severinsen's assistants, and eventually became the assistant music conductor until Johnny retired in 1992. When Jay Leno took over, Don was asked to stay with the show as the music supervisor until 1995. Just shows what a determined musician can do. Talk about an accidental incident turning the tide in someone's life! I wonder, dear reader, how accidental these incidents actually are. As Freud and probably millions of others (including the wise turtle

Oogway in *Kung Fu Panda*) have said: there are no accidents....

Let's finally track back to Orson Welles, who had become a frequent guest on Johnny's program. Johnny, too, loved magic, and, at one point during an interview, said let's go to the Magic Castle. It's a famous Hollywood nightspot where many magicians work, often close up, for and with members and guests. I've never been there, but many of my tinseltown friends have attended its shows and/or dinners.

Coincidentally, Orson and Carson never got to the Magic Castle that fateful night either. They got near it, but Carson's remark on the air must have run like wildfire through L.A., so by the time they got there the place was mobbed. They turned around, Carson dropped Welles off at his place, and then went home.

Later, Orson told Carson, that when he come back to the show the following week, "I'm going to do an extremely special psychic experiment" ... or words to that effect. Johnny was intrigued no end, but on the night that Orson promised the special surprise, Johnny was not hosting. Orson himself was the guest host, and this now great "mentalist" had a blackboard on stage. With a suitably Wellesian flourish, he asked various members of the audience to call out numbers ... and rather lengthy numbers at that.

I was appearing at a university that night, and was relaxing in my hotel room afterwards. I got a call from my road manager who said, "Turn on the Carson Show. Welles is trying to do what you do." So I turned it on, and he was just beginning this dramatic experiment. Five or six people were calling out numbers, some of which I recall being eight digits long. When he finished, it was cumbersome, because each set of numbers didn't have the same amount of digits. He proceeded to add one number that may have been in the millions to another number that may have been only five figures, but he seemed to get the total he was looking for. I don't know how in the world he was able to add all those numbers.

He then motioned towards the audience and asked a gentleman to come forward with an envelope that he had given him before the show. The gentleman sheepishly walked on stage and proceeded to open the envelope, the contents of which he showed Orson Welles. Had "The Great Orsoni" predicted the total of these numbers which had been called out spontaneously by different people in the audience?

There was a groan. A deadly silence followed the groan. The total was completely wrong.

Knowing him as I did, you could tell he was thumping upset because he had blown it. Even so, he attempted another stunt with *Tonight Show* sidekick Ed McMahon after that. It was a thought reading effect utilizing playing cards, and, dramatically, that also failed. Orson said that his hypnotic powers were not working at that time.

On the same episode the great actor Vincent Price appeared as a guest, and he had known Orson through the years. I had come to know Vincent Price through a number of television appearances, and he would warmly correspond with me, usually with hand-written notes. He walked on after these two failures and the first thing he said was, "Orson, you laid the biggest bomb of your life!" It didn't cheer Orson up, although he could have used it to take the edge off of what happened.

There's a reason Johnny Carson never again allowed Orson Welles to perform any stunt like that on his show. He would appear as a guest after that, but he was never again allowed to perform magic. It seems that many people in the audience knew what was behind this stunt. You see, the person who came forward with the envelope was a stooge of Orson Welles. As Orson was writing the numbers called out by other members of the audience, this gentleman was trying to keep up with a calculator. Although the people around him could see it, the camera would never show him, and, after he got a total, he was supposed to seal it in the envelope.

But there were three problems. First, Orson got the numbers in such a confused way. Second, there were different amounts of digits to each number. And third, this gentleman may not have known how to use a calculator that well. In any case, he ended up with the wrong total.

No one knows what happened to that stooge. Thank Heaven Orson Welles was not a marksman with a sniper's rifle, as I'm sure he would have wanted to use it. By the way, by the next day the modus operandi of what Orson did and how he did it had circulated throughout NBC. Everybody knew the story. I even got a call from Harry Blackstone Jr., the magician, who told me he was doing a show, but already knew about the Orson Welles fiasco. Word travels fast in the magician community.

Vincent Price summed it up well when he said, "Orson, you laid the biggest bomb of your life." It was the end of Citizen Welles as a great mentalist … but what a dynamic filmmaker, stage director, actor, and raconteur! He embraced the mystical arts, but, thankfully, what he told me he wanted to do that day in London he never actually did. He was going to make a one-hour magic special. But Orson was a dramatist, not a trained magician or illusionist, so he had a different way of looking at things.

What I'm about to tell you will expose no magic, destroy no illusion. You see, he was not really picking people off the street to film various segments of the magic show (as many have done since then), but using actors that he knew, who were supposed to behave like strangers. He had already done part of the bullet catch (that's a great stunt which Houdini was terrified of doing, because the great illusionist Kellar warned him, "Harry, at least a dozen have died already trying it"). Orson was intent on it, but, at that point, had only filmed the first part of the stunt: where someone was shooting the gun. Orson hadn't filmed the part where he caught the bullet.

Yes, he was planning on filming a magic show like a movie, and we all know why the magician in the movie is an interesting character ... but there is no magic, because of film editing. What makes magic work on stage never works in movies because we, the audience, know it can be faked via special effects. So Orson intended on showing an empty cabinet using all kinds of close-ups, but we all knew that once there was an edit, any magic skill is superfluous. The entire show was to be structured that way.

I'm glad it never happened, because had what he was doing with all those actors leaked out, the credibility of magic on television would have been destroyed. Today, a number of magicians are incessantly using trick photography and editing in their stunts — along with paid or unpaid stooges to fake what they are doing. It's a crying shame.

I recall many scenes of Welles as the mysterious mystifier on different shows and remember one where he had a committee of people on stage who were bearing witness to some dramatic stunt he was attempting. There, I could have pointed out to you the magicians I saw amongst them — some of whom I knew personally. They were acting, and sometimes not too well, as if they were total innocent bystanders.

Yet, if you want to know the real romance Orson had about the psychic and mysterious realms of human behavior, look at a 1949 movie he starred in. Produced and directed by Gregory Ratoff in black and white, it was not a major success, but it is the best legacy Orson left about his love of all things magical. It was called *Black Magic*, although at times it's marketed under the name *Cagliostro*.

It was a movie loosely based on a character from the middle ages who was a ruthless charlatan … ironically played by Orson Welles. Cagliostro built up a following, purported to cure people, and probably practiced some form of mesmerism. In part, the movie was based on *The Queen's Necklace*, a novel written by Alexandre Dumas in which Cagliostro played a major role. It involved intrigue with Marie Antoinette and French royalty (and was also adapted for director Richard Lester's version of *The Three Musketeers* in 1973). It was a fictional movie, but

Welles' real passion came in all the scenes involving hypnotism.

There's no doubt in my mind that Welles did much of the direction of the movie, although he was never given credit. If you saw the way the scenes were structured, they all but shouted "Welles." But it was within *Black Magic*, and Welles' performance in the hypnotism scenes, that revealed his shining passion for the mysterious. Find it if you can, and take a look. It's better than any magic, black or otherwise, that he ever attempted on television.

CHAPTER SIX
YOU ARE *NOT* GETTING SLEEPY...!

Hypnotic phenomena has always been an integral part of my career. A few years ago the BBC came to my home, partly to film my library, which is the largest in the world dealing with hypnotic phenomenon. My position on hypnosis has been written about newspapers all over the world and in medical text books. In the beginning, however, early in my career, a Dr. Harold Hanson — clinical psychologist in South Orange, NJ — approached me. His wife was expecting, and he wanted me to condition her so that she could have her child without chemical anesthetic.

He was a member of a clinical society, which, at that time, was called the Society of Clinical and Experimental Hypnosis, so I asked him why he did not go to some of the organization's most prominent members. He informed me that he had, but they were not able to influence his wife. He had seen me perform, and felt I could work with her. The meetings with her were successful, and, at least to some degree, there was a minimal amount of chemical anesthesia used in her childbirth.

That was the beginning of a long association with Dr. Hanson. In fact, he gave me an office in his suite, and turned over patients he felt I could help with my hypnotic skills. Understand, at this point, I had not graduated from Seton Hall University (where I majored in psychology) and was also performing.

At the end of eight years, my performing schedule became so hectic that I had to pass on working with his patients, but I saw some very dramatic scenarios during that time. There were individuals who were afraid of heights, but would soon join me standing at the edge of a six-story building. There were individuals who were claustrophobic, but were finally able to enter an elevator with no one with them, or sit amidst a crowd at church, and on and on.

But, as the years passed and my work with hypnotic techniques developed, I began to notice that I could get results with people who didn't seem to go into a deep trance. They were not what we call somnambulistic subjects, or even medium level subjects. That used to bother me, and I discussed it with Dr. Hanson. He was familiar with hypnosis. We couldn't come to a conclusion, but I had a suspicion. What could I do if I didn't hypnotize anybody or put them in a formal trance ... just suggest things? Could I get results?

I decided to experiment, and it marked a remarkable evolution in my career. I discovered that, by pure suggestion, I was able to cause fully awake people to believe as deeply as those who were apparently under deep levels of hypnosis. Somehow, I had embraced the real secret of hypnosis — that of a fake prestige relationship — and made my suggestions convincing.

Today it's nothing for me to walk up to a wide awake subject on stage, gaze at them for five or six seconds, then ask them to get out of their chair … and they can't. Or I'll ask someone their name, and the audience will see them gagging, unable to talk.

I inevitably came to the conclusion that the "hypnotic trance" doesn't exist — no trace of it exists at all. No one is in an altered state of consciousness, either higher or lower. No one is in any semi-lull of consciousness. Relaxation has nothing to do with it, except the belief on the part of the subject that relaxation is going to make them more suggestible.

But the difficulty in administering pure suggestion is that, for most practioners, i.e. hypnotists, it's not theatrically convincing enough for subjects (and/or witnesses) so they need the charade of the hypnotic induction technique. You know, that old routine: "you're getting sleepy, sleepy, drowsy, drowsy," and so forth. It's all to make the person believe the suggestions about to be given are going to succeed.

I've stepped over all that, setting the traditional methods aside, and am often able to create response to what I say almost spontaneously. Psychologists have often left my program fascinated, after I would take an entire group of people, sit at the piano, and play the song *Sleep* (it was a theme song of the late Fred Waring, a famous orchestra and chorus leader) … only to have them all do just that.

One of my fondest memories was performing *Sleep* at Carnegie Hall with an orchestra behind me, while subjects were toppling off their chairs, lying on the floor, or slumbering over each other all around us. The song alone had suggested the feeling of forty winks, even though there was no trance at all.

With this in mind, many states have abandoned laws about hypnosis — including Kansas, which had a law reading you couldn't hypnotize anyone in public (let alone swallow snakes or eat the heads off lizards, etc.). That regulation went back to the carnival days at the turn of the century.

But when my findings became clear that there was no trance, the law became frivolous. In one dramatic situation, as a reporter wrote about the next day, a unanimous vote took place to abandon the law. Writers said that I had zapped the state legislature. Laws controlling hypnosis became less effective. In truth, they were literally worthless.

I'm not saying people are faking when they're treated by hypnotists. It's just that they're not really in a "trance." In fact, it's a wise hypnotist who knows who's hypnotizing whom! The hypnotist believes that they have their subject in a trance, but suggestion alone can have a truly reassuring, and sometimes even an actual healing, quality about it.

Then are all hypnotists fake? No ... although I recall when a reporter called me to recount how they volunteered for a stage hypnotist in Las Vegas, and how the performer didn't even realize that his stage subjects weren't responding to the suggestions, were totally in their own control, and even whispering amongst themselves.

In recent years I've offered $100,000 to anyone who could prove hypnotic trance. When my suspicion started growing about the nature of hypnotic phenomenon in the 1960's and 70's, an experimental psychologist by the name of T.X. Barber caused an uproar amongst researchers when he suggested that there really was no hypnotic trance.

Our meeting was a charming experience. I had invited T.X. to give a lecture for the Association of Advanced Hypnosis, a group I helped form with the author and hypnosis expert Harry Arons. Afterwards, we practically sat on the living room floor amongst all the guests, sharing with each other how we came to the conclusion that there really was no hypnotic state or trance at all.

But it wasn't always that way. In the early years of television, hypnosis was popular because we saw people responding to amusing and sometimes outrageous suggestions. But along came a televised magician who purports that he's going to hypnotize a whole hotel dining room of people. They're all gathered there, sitting at different tables, and he begins to very briefly administer some mumbo-jumbo, and, lo and behold, people throughout the room seem to slumber off into a hypnotic trance.

But nothing is done with them. The scenario ends there as if he's achieved what he claimed he was going to do. Oh, parenthetically, might I add that a waiter came through with a tray of dishes and collapsed on the floor. To the astute psychology student, that was the give away that the whole thing was a fraud, and that nobody was under hypnosis. They were just play-acting, having made an agreement to deceive the audience into thinking that the performer was creating the scene with innocent subjects.

Innocent? No. They were all told to make believe they were undergoing hypnosis. None of them went into any kind of state of high suggestibility. The clue, my dear Watson, being the person serving food. Common sense ruins the scenario. First of all, would a person come in to serve drinks and/or food while an entire group of people were being hypnotized? To say you didn't know this was going to happen is pretty pathetic, because when you've got a TV crew putting together a production, you make sure there are not going to be any interruptions ... let alone a waiter who risked disturbing the process.

In addition, there was no food to be served at that time, since the hypnotist was going to perform. Finally, the server falling with a full tray is pretty far fetched. Unless a hypnotist is supremely secure, you really can't make a person do what he doesn't want to do.

Did the waiter not know what was going on? Obviously untrue. Is the waiter going to serve in spite of the people being hypnotized? Obviously unacceptable. Did the waiter somehow go into a trance and collapse? Difficult to believe. Would the production company allow individuals to be injured by flying glass or shattered crockery? Does anyone in their right mind think that a production company would allow such irresponsible actions to take place, opening them to a wide array of lawsuits?

Bottom line, folks, if you saw this scene as I did, you saw nothing to do with hypnosis. You saw a play between an audience that was faking things and a performer that was perpetrating the fraud. Elementary, my dear Watson.

Performing as I do before university and educational groups (as well as in theaters, state fairs, private parties, corporate events, and what have you), students will often discuss events with me events that have intrigued them through the years. At various after-parties, receptions, or even in auditorium lobbies, they feel I might be able to add some clarity or perspective to things they've seen or heard of.

A number of them had seen a TV stunt where a hypnotist went to a campsite and apparently lured a man into a deep hypnotic trance for literally hours. He returned and awakened the subject, who was stunned that so many hours of the night had passed. Interestingly enough, two of the TV viewers were graduate students preparing for a masters in psychology. Their questioning of the situation was astute, despite the fact that they were not authorities on hypnosis.

They knew my position on hypnosis, namely that there is no trance, special condition, sub-level of thinking, or special altered state, but they didn't need to be me to accurately analyze the scenario of the stunt on television. If anyone thinks that an individual can be approached by a stranger and, with no pre-arrangement, pre-planning, or pre-agreement, go into a mindless trance for hours, that "anyone" might want to hear about some swamp land I have for sale.

One would have to get permission to attempt such a stunt, otherwise they would run the risk of being sued when the individual was awakened many hours later. So, if one looks at it with just a sense of logic, it could not possibly have taken place in the manner in which the illusion was presented. The entranced man was aware of what was going on all the time, and the surprise or confusion at the end of the stunt was more fabricated than real.

One of the most dramatic scenarios that I heard of, but did not see, was that of a hypnotist who was going to train businessmen with some kind of mind development lecture. Inevitably, the hypnotist somehow got these subjects so deeply entranced that he was able to take them to a bank, and get the men to rob it. What had been presented was a business training session that turned into a pseudo-robbery by the hypnotist.

I was asked, was such a thing possible? Could such a thing be done? For the record, the answer is very simply no. Communicated a bit less simply: absolutely not. I've lectured, written, testified under oath, and been involved in enough legislative situations to speak with some expertise on hypnotic phenomenon. It is ludicrous to think that people could be made to commit a crime through hypnotic techniques, since the persons are conscious and cognizant throughout any such procedure.

Could this scenario for television presentation take place? That answer is yes. Did I just contradict myself? Nope. Let's forget, for the moment, about con-magicians who make secret agreements with people to play along — deceiving and betraying the trust of the viewers — because there's another way this could be done. As Shakespeare said, "All the world's a stage, and all the men and women merely players."

With media saturating our lives, millions feel that they're going to get, as Andy Warhol said, their fifteen minutes of fame. Now into some of those people's lives comes a person who suggests that they're going beyond the framework of a business setting into a bank. If there is no overt request just to playact and move along with this, it can still work if the performer of this stunt is persuasive enough to encourage the people to go along with him. After all, there are cameras everywhere, so why not proceed with this experience? They are all certain they will not be harmed or in trouble, so why not go along? Might be fun.

Consequently, a sense of theater is being created, and they are now a group of "hypnotized bank robbers." The operative word in that sentence is "group." Hear me: a group, not one person, who each is aware that others are participating. If there's going to be any real trouble, it's going to be others who will testify to the fact that this was a planned scenario. No, you're not being made to do this by yourself. In a group there's less responsibility, and more play-acting. One episode of any "reality show" involving a bunch of "strangers" thrown together in a house, apartment, kitchen, runway, modeling agency, or wilderness contains ample evidence of somewhat self-conscious, self-indulgent, and self-aware "drama."

So, in holding up the bank, there really is an implied, albeit pretty clear, understanding within the group that they're going to make "good television." Could they then be, as a result of this, made to go up and rob some stranger on the street ... with no cameras there watching, and no one with them? Ah, that would be the prime test, wouldn't it?

What do you think? Just remember that everyone who's ever appeared to be in a hypnotic trance is not only totally conscious and awake, but aware of everything that's going on. The true subject feels a tremendous, compelling, and compulsion to respond. Real hypnotized people are not play-acting, but still they're consciously aware of what's going on.

So much for the present. Now I'm going to share with you one of the most dramatic secrets of past stage hypnotists. Not the legitimate ones, but the fake ones. In describing this to you, I must warn you never to attempt this, for it is seriously dangerous. Understand, too, that it has nothing to do with the power of suggestion, hypnosis, or whatever you may call it. It is a ruse to create the illusion that a person has slumbered into a deep and conscious trance.

In the old days, the hypnotists may have used this to handle annoying volunteers who didn't want to go along with their fakery. What did the hypnotist do? He simply stepped in front of the subject, touched him on the face, and shouted "sleep!" The subject would then slump in his chair or even collapse to the floor. What you didn't know is that the "hypnotist" pressed the subject's carotid vessels — shutting off blood circulation for a few seconds, creating unconsciousness.

It's a classic martial art technique, commonplace in judo, karate, and jujitsu. It's also dangerous and not to be trifled with, although certain self-proclaimed "Masters" still try to impress the gullible with it. But it's nothing that ever should be done, although it was done on stage in the past many, many times. I've heard of bad acts killing vaudeville, but it's never a good idea to hurt your audience. As Monty Python said, "Never kill a customer."

———◆———

But I truly don't think of my audience as "customers." I think of them as friends. In fact, I don't really see much difference between the people I entertain today and my young schoolmates when I started all those years ago. My use of audience members has always been an integral part of my performance. As I've often said, there really are no footlights between me and the audience.

It's their thoughts I'm perceiving, and, when I demonstrate some of the comedy and drama of "hypnotic" suggestion, I use only audience members who are sufficiently suggestible to respond to my influence. Of course on television, whether it's thought-reading or suggestion, I often use celebrities as well. But, in each and every case, these are not stooges … no Peter Sellers in the rafters, as it were. My subjects are not people who are faking, nor are they people who are secretly collaborating to create a dishonest experience.

For instance, a few years ago at the CTV Network in Canada, a nighttime series starred comedian/raconteur Mike Bullard. The show had remarkably high ratings, and it was my privilege to work with

Mike on many occasions. One particular scenario has become a major story in my career and has been recounted by Mike Bullard many times.

The show was broadcast live in front of a few hundred, highly responsive, people, but when I arrived at the studio, I was told that Mike was preoccupied. It has always been my policy in order to avoid contact with show hosts prior to taping, lest there be suspicions of pre-arrangement or other chicanery, so I did not see Mike before the show. The crew went on to explain that within the past forty-eight hours Mike's car had been stolen, and he was deeply stressed over it.

As it got closer to show time, I became very introspective. I always keep to myself before a television show. In a regular concert, before I go on stage for my standard two hours and thirty minutes, I need to be alone for approximately an hour. But as the director alerted me that I would be going on shortly, I said, in essence, "Listen, I may divert from the test that I'm planning to do because there's something that I'd like to discuss of a very serious nature."

They didn't ask me what it was or what area it would cover. They trusted my spontaneous way of working, having worked with me before. I walked on, Mike and I exchanged humorous pleasantries (as he has a great sense of humor), but then I brought up the car robbery. Here my memory a little vague. He may have suggested that I could solve the crime with my abilities, but if he did, he didn't mean it as a literal remark or want to put me on the spot.

However, I took advantage of the moment. I turned to the camera, looked directly into it, and addressed my remarks, not to the millions watching, but to an unknown person. A person I felt certain was watching. The person who stole the car.

I made it very clear to him, and I knew it was a he, that he was watching. In fact, I was certain he had been riveted to the show the past two nights because of his crime, and he was not going to be able to take his eyes off me.

But that's only the beginning. I said that within two days he would deliver that car to a street I named which was in the area. I specified the exact time frame and the location, then turned away from the camera. Mike and audience were nonplussed, to say the least, that I would take such a chance in dealing with a person who could possibly be violent.

Nevertheless, the rest of the show went well. I left that evening and headed home the next day. It wasn't long before I got an array of calls. All hell had broken loose. Mike Bullard's car was found … on the city block that I said it would be, and within the two hour period that I had admonished the criminal to return it. The bottom line is that my calculations were correct. The car thief was watching the show, my personalizing hit home, and this robber responded in exactly the way that I designed.

This is one reality show that happened for real without camera trickery, scripting, or editing, and it carried into real life. If only this sort of thing would happen more often…!

———◆———

In 2008, while touring Canada, I experienced an unnerving set of circumstances, for which I have no explanation. But one thing I am sure about … it was no coincidence. It was far more than coincidence.

During this particular tour, I was featuring an experiment that dealt with the responses brought forth by a volunteer. The only thing I wrote ahead of time were my thoughts. I sealed them in an envelope, and they were given to either the theater manager or an usher — someone in the audience who could be relied on to open the envelope at the proper time.

One night, a gentleman came forward and gave us all his word that he did not tamper with the envelope and did not know what was in it. Amongst other things, I asked him come up with the name of someone who was significant in his life. He mentioned a first name. Then he was astonished when he opened the envelope to find that I had written the same name that he said when he came up on stage.

I had predicted the thoughts he was going to come forth with. As I always do, because of the personal interest to my audience and myself, I will ask how he came to pick the name that no one knew except himself … and myself. His name was his brother.

Needless to say, when I decided on this first name earlier in my dressing room while preparing for the show, I had no thought of anyone's brother. I just made a decision that I was going to project this first name into the mind of someone in the audience. But when he said it was "his brother," I detected something in the phraseology. I said to him, "What do you mean, your brother?" And he said that his brother had passed away eight years before.

The next night, in another Canadian city, many hundreds of miles from the previous one, I presented the same test as part of my concert. The envelope had been given to someone, not by me, but by an usher sometime earlier. The person was asked again, just as the night before, to pick some first name, but this time, also to pick some date in his life, as well as some other items I had decided upon. When he opened the envelope, I was correct on all three accounts, and that included a first name (a name I had decided upon earlier in the day).

In each case, I asked why he made such final decisions. The date was of some trip he had made in the past. The first name was … you guessed it … the name of his brother. I paused for a moment, remembering the night before. I also realized that he had used the word "was." I asked, "What do you mean, was?" You guessed it again. His brother had passed away eight or nine years before. Two nights in a row, people I had never met used names I never thought about before, but both were brothers who had passed away around eight years prior.

Mental projection or prophecy? You decide, because, as you've read, I've already decided. To paraphrase Nietzsche, "When you look into an abyss, sometimes the abyss also looks into you." Just as the body can react to training and exercise in ways that even surprise the athlete, so can your mind, if you exercise it well enough.

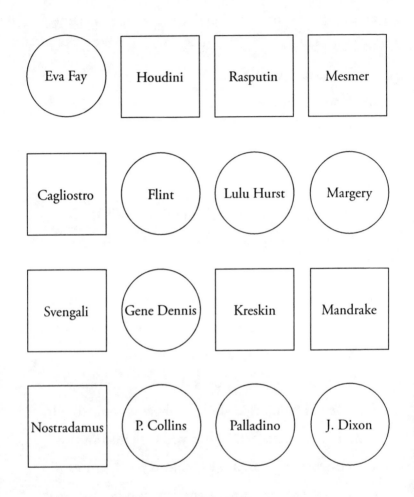

YOU WILL FIND YOURSELF
DRAWN TO "KRESKIN"

CHAPTER SEVEN
MY CHECKERED PAST

Eventually, one of the most important parts of my concerts was a scenario one critic in Pittsburgh described as "watching a play on the stage." What was unusual about this mystery play was that the solution was different every show.

This portion of my program is the lynchpin in the plot of *The Great Buck Howard*, and any of you who have seen this 2009 film are now familiar with the signature of my performance. For well over fifty years, the scenario is simply this: I submit my pay for the performance over to a committee of five or six audience members, picked by chance. Another group from the audience, often with theater officials or security people, escort me from the theater, so I have no way of seeing what is taking place.

The committee then takes my check and hides it —literally hides it, anywhere in the entire theatre … so long as it is physically accessible and there is no danger to anyone involved. The committee then returns to the stage and I am called back in. Our agreement is simple. Should I fail to locate the check by reading the thoughts of the hiding committee, I forfeit my fee. And by the way, the committee does not speak to me. They do not communicate with me in any way, shape or form, outside of their thoughts and proximity.

Have I failed? You're damn right I have … nine times! One was in New Zealand where I forfeited some fifty-one thousand dollars. Another was at a Texas college where I found an envelope and was walking toward the stage when someone in the audience shouted out, "Make sure it's *your* check, Kreskin." I froze, realizing something was wrong. When I opened the envelope, it wasn't there. It turns out the committee had hidden a number of envelopes in different places and nobody, even the committee, knew which envelope contained my pay. I had been cheated. I could have argued the point and certainly demanded the check but I was so discouraged and disheartened that I let it slide. The audience booed the committee.

That night, I was asked to come to the University President's home. Within minutes after my two-and-a-half hour concert's standing ovation (which I was proud to receive), the President had received scores of calls complaining that I had been cheated. Even while visiting him, the calls continued. One of the priceless possessions of my career are the pages and pages of an "Apology Petition" — with the signatures of hundreds of students — that I received from the University weeks later. In truth, I did not fail, for I had no one's thoughts I could legitimately read.

Another heartbreaking forfeiture took place in the state of Connecticut. I had returned to a high school to present a public concert because a previous one had been so successful. Before the show, I was invited to a private party, which the head of the Psychology department, the Psychology teacher, some other teachers, and some specially selected students attended. I was unsettled at the party — courteous to everyone but truly disturbed about something. My road manager kept asking me what was wrong and I kept saying, "I don't know." There was just … something … wrong.

The night of the show will never be erased from my mind. In front of a full, immensely enthusiastic audience, came the "check test." On the committee was a Psychology teacher, a math teacher, and a couple of students. When I returned to the theatre to search, one of the committee members was following me out towards the lobby of the theatre. I couldn't figure out why, because, when I opened the door to the lobby, it didn't seem right, so I came back in.

Back and forth I went until I finally gave up. At that moment, there was unrest in the theatre. It didn't seem like it was criticism of my failure, but it seemed like a brewing storm. Indeed, the mother of a young lady who I had dated earlier in my high school days was in the audience, and word got back to me twenty-four hours later about how infuriated she was.

It seemed that a number of people in the audience somehow detected that I was being cheated, and enough people had been let in on this fact that word had gotten around. Oh, yes, that night I failed, but...! It turns out that this show was a fundraiser ... not for all the students, but for a select group of student skiers who wanted to go all the way to Colorado who, with the influence of the Psychology teacher, had been told to think of the wrong hiding place!

I realized at the intermission that I had been cheated. Days later, I was in another part of the country. I received a call from a national press dispatch. The information that I had been taken advantage of and duped unfairly had gotten to them, and for some strange reason the Psychology professor was not available for comment for a number of days. It seemed as if he had left town. In some way, karma being what it is, I expect that he paid his price.

So, although almost half of the failures were not because of my inability to read the thoughts of the committee, but because of cheating, I was still unsuccessful nine times. They were traumatic failures. You can probably tell that I still really haven't gotten over them. Even though it was "only" nine times out of thousands of performances, it's never fun giving away your salary. So I made a decision that should I ever fail a tenth time, I would cease to do the test.

I still dwell on the legitimate failures, as perhaps you can tell, and distinctly remember the one that had nothing to do with the committee. It had to do with my own reasoning. I am a big fan of Sherlock Holmes and sympathize with him in Sir Arthur Conan Doyle's famous story, *A Scandal in Bohemia*, where the great detective's reasoning is bested by the person he called "The Woman," Irene Adler.

My "scandal" took place in Atlantic City, New Jersey. It was a performance for the American Medical Association College of Surgeons. The room was packed —so filled, in fact, that folding chairs were set up for overflow doctors who wanted to attend. Time came for the check test. As I can recount in almost every situation and setting, this gigantic room was dead silent as I walked through it. Every step was weighed and observed by this audience — an audience of scientists and medically trained minds.

My "Irene Adler" was a woman in the audience who I asked to get out of her chair. She wasn't sitting on the check. It was a folding chair, and I turned it over but the check simply wasn't there. I had to sit down. I felt maybe I had a poor mind-reading subject, so I asked another committee member just to follow me and concentrate.

It was perplexing. I circled around the auditorium, came back to "The Woman" again, and again, and again. Some four or five times I found myself at the same destination. I turned the chair over again. I tried to find any folding of cloth or wrappings around the chair … anything that could hide a check. I was absolutely flummoxed.

I finally made a decision that I dreaded making…. "Ladies and gentlemen, I can't go on. I failed." There was dead silence. The president up on the dais said, "Well, of course, Kreskin, we'll pay you." I said, "No. I can't jeopardize my career. This is not a magic act. Things are not done over. I failed."

PS: They so enjoyed my program that they asked if I could turn my fee over to some cause or charity, and, being a graduate of Seton Hall University, it was donated to the educational department.

But back to the search. Oh yes, I had successfully perceived the thoughts of the committee member. The Woman did have to get out of the chair. I was correct in picking up the chair. The problem is that my mind and reason interfered. The check was under The Woman. It was under the chair. I was literally standing an eighth of an inch from the check.

While I was out of the room, the committee, ingeniously and fairly, decided to move all the chairs aside, roll up the rug, and put the check under where this lady was sitting. Then they just rolled the rug back, put the chair in place, she sat down and that was that. I had the right thought … I simply had not gone far enough. I don't intend to make that mistake again, my dear Watson.

Ah, but aside from the nine setbacks, the successes are some of the dramatic moments of my life. After all, I have succeeded somewhere around six thousand times. Can you imagine walking into a banquet hall at the internationally famous Waldorf Astoria, at a dinner in honor of comedian supreme Bob Hope, and finding yourself on the dais? Bob Hope, that American institution, said that he had seen me on television but never knew I did anything like the search that occurred that night.

You could hear a pin drop. The room was filled with writers, radio personalities, and TV stars, who watched as I kept lifting a large tray off the table in front of Hope. I believe it contained a half-carved fowl of some sort. I gather that if a person at the table wanted more, they could just move the plate over and scoop out some further food. But the check wasn't under the plate. I got flustered. I turned to the committee member who was following me and said, "Do you really know where this is?"

She had a right to be indignant. A perfect right. She said, "Of course I do, all of us agreed to where it would be hidden!" Sheepishly I realized the scolding was justified, and felt slightly embarrassed. Still, I picked up the plate a couple more times. Finally I looked at her and said, "Oh my God, no!" I took off my tuxedo jacket, rolled up my sleeve, and shoved my hand into the turkey. They had buried it deep within the stuffing! To this day I can intimately recall the texture....

I also remember the time when I walked through a gymnasium containing a few thousand students, parents, and my check. I grabbed a gentleman in a suit and started pulling him towards the stage area, where there was a platform. As we were walking down the aisle, I said the word "gun," and thought, what possessed me to do such a thing?

When we got in front of the audience, however, I opened the gentleman's jacket. He was a plainclothes detective, and there it was, a shoulder holster. I then enacted a scenario that I don't think I would ever do in any other circumstance. Guns are not my thing, but that night I took the weapon out of his holster, turned the barrel of the gun towards my eyes. They had taken tweezers and slowly fed the rolled check down the barrel of the gun. Now I know how James Bond feels at the start of every 007 movie (except *Quantum of Solace*, which didn't have the trademark gun barrel opening sequence).

This check-finding climax is not just nerve-wracking for me and the audience, you know. As a matter of fact, the first time I appeared at Carnegie Hall (which was, of course, a red letter day in my career), when it came to the moment of the check test, a couple of dozen people walked out of the theater. They did not leave the show. They came back afterwards. The audience probably wondered why. I knew why. All of those people were personal friends who had attended programs before. Therefore, they were highly unnerved by the check test, because they knew the turmoil I went through.

Two of my road managers, who were always out of the theater during the check test for obvious reasons, would always become extremely apprehensive as more than a few minutes went by in my search. They knew I was in trouble. So many of my Carnegie Hall friends had attended performances where I was literally on the verge of throwing in the towel ... but for some reason kept at it until I finally found the check.

In 2008, an entry on the internet proposed to "expose" the "secret" of locating my pay check. A self-styled magician and magical expert titled his entry "Magic of Kreskin Explained." For a whole minute we considered filing a lawsuit (and we would have had a field day), but we realized that the web is really an example of the Wild West uncontrolled. One could spend years, and millions of dollars, addressing every lie written about them on the net. Let me share with you the modus operandi that he reveals, and perhaps you will get a chuckle out of it. I certainly did.

According to the explanation, before the performance instructions are given to a confederate (doesn't that ring a bell) to present and hide the check in a very specific way. The check must be sealed in an envelope. It must be hidden somewhere accessible and it must be within a hundred yards of the performance area. The confederate must know where the check is, and, are you ready, the check *must be written on a one-inch thick piece of iron.*

I hope, my dear reader, you have not fallen out of your chair. According to the "secret," the slab of iron is apparently the key to the affect, for when the attempt is made to locate the check, a large electronic magnet hidden beneath my shirt is switched on, attracting the metal check. The performer, I suppose that's yours truly, obviously is feeling "pulled" and simply follows the direction of the attraction.

My dear reader, can you imagine how many watches I would stop, and how many necklaces, earrings, hair clips, et al, would go flying? This scenario would be a natural to test on *Mythbusters*. Better yet, it seems perfect for *Saturday Night Live* ... maybe on a night when John Malkovich is hosting.

Which brings us back to *The Great Buck Howard*. It was a remarkable experience to find that one of my road managers, Sean McGinley, who had traveled with me in 1994, had lovingly wrote and directed this tale of an extraordinary entertainer. The story had absolutely nothing to do with yours truly, of course, but the character ... well, his character and abilities are a different story...!

Buck Howard, and his spitting image John Malkovich, so totally captured my persona, as well as much of the content of my performances, that I had a serious case of déjà vu watching them. Telepathic abilities, check. Hypnotic techniques, check. Use of the piano, double-check! I can tell you that the setting of the stage when Buck Howard is performing is exactly the same setting that I require in the second half of my concerts. They even got my infamous teeth-rattling, shoulder-threatening hand-shake down (what can I tell you? A lot of energy is required for my work).

As far as Buck's temperament, negativeness, and disagreeable qualities, I'd like to think that the freedom of creating that story is far removed from yours truly. But the key point of the movie is my check test, and the question remains in both life and the movie: is it legit? In the movie, the use of electronic devices is seriously suggested. It's even suggested that Buck had an assistant who followed him in another plane and planted himself in the audience of each show.

I am most pleased with the statement made by the producers when the movie concludes that not only is the title character inspired by yours truly, but I've never used such devices or trickery in my work.

No, I don't use secret electronic devices. No, I don't have secret assistants and plants in the audience. I have too much respect for the performers who inspired me to take such an easy way out. But I'll be honest … perhaps there are some times during my trials and tasks that I entertain, maybe just for a fleeting nanosecond, the wish that I had something which would make things easier.

As an example, let me tell you about one of my greatest searches … not for a mere check, but for a full-fledged human being. Some years ago, when Robin Leach had the TV series *Lifestyles of the Rich and Famous* (1984 – 1995), I offered another segment to the program beyond touring my house.

The producers said, "We've already given the amount of time that we give each celebrity, but what have you in mind?"

When I told them they asked if I was kidding.

I said of course not.

They said if this fails, we won't show it.

I said yes, you will.

In all my years on television — the more than a hundred shows with Mike Douglas, the eighty-eight Johnny Carson shows, the nearly one hundred Merv Griffin shows — one thing was clear: on live television there's no turning back. The credibility of what I do is based on the fact that a failure remains a failure — not to be done over or corrected.

I was driven to the Tavern on the Green, just off Central Park in New York City. There I was met by the prominent New York Post columnist, Cindy Adams, a couple of other city figures, and a number of police cars. The challenge was simply this: somewhere in the entire city of Manhattan was Robin Leach. I had to find him.

Cindy and the others focused their thoughts on Robin's location. I spoke only to the driver of a limo, telling him which streets to go down, among other things. On a couple of occasions, there was slight panic, as I was sending him down a one-way street … the wrong way. The police were following us, but it was hard to do much, since they weren't in front of us. It was the blind leading the skeptical.

But that changed, because, in less than an hour, I came to a point where I decided we needed to leave the limo. I led everyone into a building and walked to the elevator. I'll tell you, it had been a very frustrating search, and I responded by finally slamming my hand against the wall next to the elevator and walking out of the building.

It just seemed to me like this was as far as I could go … still, something wasn't right. I looked at the building from outside and realized how tall it was, then went back in with a little more confidence. The elevator, by its floor number buttons, obviously didn't cover the entire building. In my mind, Robin Leach was hiding at a higher level. We took the elevator up to the highest floor it could take us.

There we found another elevator, and went to a higher floor. I led the group, camera crew and all, to a large swimming pool area. The whole floor seemed empty, save for the water. I just stood there looking at the swimming pool … staring at the pool. I'm sure the committee and the camera crew was wondering what was going on. It was obvious that Robin Leach was not in the pool. There was nobody in the pool.

Finally, after a few minutes, I looked up and there was a door at the very end of the pool. We walked across the area, opened the door, and discovered it was the entrance to a bar. Inside, there were people cleaning glasses, assembling tables, and the like. As I approached the bar, I saw a man leaning over there. His face wasn't visible, and I didn't know if he was sober or not, but his form was familiar.

I'm sure you've already guessed: it was Robin Leach. I had found him in less than an hour. He opened a bottle of champagne to celebrate. A camera crew member mentioned to him that I was outside this room for a few minutes staring at the swimming pool. I told him, "Robin, even I'm perplexed at what I was doing." He showed a sign of excitement in his face and explained that when the camera crew notified him that the search was to begin, he decided that it would be dramatic if I found him swimming in the pool.

He had changed into his bathing suit and swam for almost half an hour. But as time went by, he became waterlogged, got up, dried off, changed his clothes, and decided on the bar. But for almost thirty minutes he was in the pool I kept staring at, envisioning him there, though not to be seen.

Now if only he had been a paycheck in New Zealand, or Texas, or Connecticut, or Atlantic City…!

CHAPTER EIGHT

TRICKS OF THE TRADE

It's very common today to see a stage mind-reader, but what you may not realize is that the techniques you're seeing have been lifted from older, time-tested mediums. In one touring, so-called, show, people write questions or comments on cards, which are sealed in envelopes. The envelopes are put into a bowl, and, one at a time, the mentalist (or mind-reader or psychic) holds the envelope to his head and gets readings.

Johnny Carson and I often talked about this when he was hosting *The Tonight Show*. As you've read, he even often did a comedic satire of this act, playing "Carnac the Magnificent." That's only natural, because the standard mind-reading act really makes no sense. If a person is holding an envelope to his head is supposed to be communicating with a loved one, why would he have to hold the envelope? If the person is reading someone's thoughts in the audience, why would he have to hold the envelope?

The answer is very simple. It's because he's reading what is inside the sealed envelope. There are at least a dozen ways of seeing into an envelope and reading a message without breaking open the envelope. Sometimes the performer may even be blindfolded, but, in spite of the fact that he doesn't appear to be able to see, he can see everything, and, through certain tactics, sometimes using chemicals, has made the envelope transparent.

However, all these areas of trickery and their methodology can be set aside, and you can fake a "Kreskin" in a much easier way. You just need two things. A son or a daughter twelve years old or older, and two rented rooms. You then invite people to come to your séance-like presentation. Set it up so they can pay by credit card if you (or they) want. You see, that's the key.

All you need is to have your son or daughter in the other room with a computer. Give them some basic information, such as the name of the person who signs the credit card payment, and you'll be surprised how your son or daughter can probably come up with a bunch of information about the person who came to the show. And there you sit with information your son or daughter gave you just before you went on. Congratulations. You are now a touring mindreader.

⟽⟾◆⟻⟾

There are legends built around Voodoo. While some consider it a religion, to be respected as such, it is interesting to note that in places like Haiti, many of the people who practice Voodoo are also Roman Catholic. Somehow they have adjusted to the apparent contradictions in the religious thinking of both practices. Any true horror movie fan is aware of the severe side of Voodooism, of course. Some tales are built on folklore, others on reality. Even outside cinemas, there are multitudes of people who believe that a spell can be cast.

But for the sake of entertainment, let's examine how this can be done. Can a person die if they have been victim of a Voodoo witch-doctor's spell? As a cynic and a skeptic of some claims, especially those of spirit mediums and the like, I still answer the question as "yes." It can work, but not for the reason that you might think. Could simply a belief cause a person to die? Probably, on rare occasions.

Voodoo ceremonies, whether held in tropic settings or modern society, can be very dramatic. There was a time when yours truly was appearing as an entertainer on a cruise ship. One night I was able to leave the ship when it had docked in Haiti, and was brought to an evening Voodoo ceremony. The dancing there became almost hypnotic, and almost exhausting to watch. The same people continued with rhythmic motion — almost detached from their surroundings. Even the memory of that night is almost mesmerizing. It certainly is distracting me from the main point.

Let's get back to causing someone to die through Voodooistic means. The reason that people have died when cursed is because of their belief. An experimental psychologist reported this to me in great detail. He said that when the individual and families learn of the curse, those who totally embrace and accept the idea simply make it so. The victim accepts it, lying on a cot in the house with the family sitting around him, waiting. No food is given or taken. The family's resignation simply allows the curse victim to starve to death.

I am not happy about this, but I'm also not shocked. It's all a part of human nature, which I've learned through my years of study and experience. As example, here is a dramatic test that I have presented on television. It dealt with the transference of thoughts, and the response of the person targeted as the object of the thoughts. Usually my scenario involves two strangers from the studio audience, or a stranger and a celebrity.

The stranger sits with their back to us. Meanwhile the celebrity is shown a doll — described as a Voodoo doll. A needle is given to the celebrity, and, often with my back to the celebrity I request that he (or she) place the needle into a certain part of the doll's body — be it the arm, neck, leg, or whatever.

The climax is quite dramatic, for as the person plunges the needle, I often react by grabbing that area of my body that reflects their choice. But attention is almost instantly drawn to the other side of the stage, where the stranger, not seeing what was done, is reacting in pain at exactly the area where the celebrity plunged the pin on the doll.

Oh, by the way, in recent years magicians have purported to show this as a stunt, but as usual, they went too far. I saw one where someone plunged a needle into a doll, and the individual responded, but then the magician showed the needle to the person experiencing pain, and continued to push it into various other parts of the doll, whereby the individual felt pain in each of these areas (knee, neck, shoulder, right arm, left arm, whatever).

If you happen to see this act, or one like it, understand that the best part is how instantly the subject reacts. It's hard to accept this as legitimate when all these quick plunges are being experienced just as instantly. Anyone with any knowledge of this technique knows it's a set-up situation with an actor "playing" the innocent victim. It's all for the benefit of audiences who only know Voodoo from seeing the likes of *Indiana Jones and the Temple of Doom*.

———◆———

Some years ago at a magician's convention, a performer who proclaimed himself a mentalist decided to do the "Kreskin test." Not only was he to find a person or object amongst this audience of professional and amateur magicians, but he allowed himself to be blindfolded throughout the test. It was a dramatic, colorful scenario. It didn't convince the magicians that he was reading thoughts, but he did complete the challenge, tests, and search that he set out to enact.

The fact that he could see even though he was blindfolded was not important. As I've said, many magicians are blindfolded and they can still see everything. But this particular one did complete the search. To be honest, he probably could have done this even if he couldn't see, because there were electronic devices in use. In this case, an earpiece, through which he was told everything he needed to know to complete the test.

A gentleman I've known for many years, Tony Spina, who ran a magic emporium selling tricks, gimmicks, and illusions to profession and amateur magicians, had an associate, Irv Tannen, who I also came to know very well. Irv was very protective of my career and very defensive when some magicians questioned what I did. But they both related to me how they had sold the electronic equipment to this self-styled mentalist, and that the equipment that they sold then is still for sale today, and used by performers who are supposedly doing something "Kreskin."

———⊨◆⊨———

Here's a method that anyone can use to show friends a Kreskin test. Invite your friends over. The more the merrier. You now can say that you've seen *The Great Buck Howard*, and are so fascinated with Kreskin's telepathic ability that you're going to imitate it. Inform your friends to choose one person, without your knowledge. Before they do, you walk into a closet. Then four or five people need to go over and touch the chosen one on the shoulder, to establish that is the person.

Everybody then separates, and stands around the room. Then someone needs to retrieve. Then it's your turn: you walk slowly around the room slowly, holding your head in apparent meditation, and finally you come to one person, and after pausing a bit, proceed to put your hands on the person and say that this is the individual that they decided upon.

You will always succeed (except in one instance) How? Cheat. Simply have your cell phone on your person and preassign a friend you can trust. When you're in the closet, set your cell phone to "vibrate." Your confederate knows the target. When you get closer to the person, your secret assistant sets off the cell phone. Ta-da!

To show you how far electronics has entered the mystery age — and really has cheated the audience — some years ago a psychic performer was on the radio in California and when people called in, proceeded to tell their names and other bits of information about them. Listeners might have been impressed, but anyone who knows radio or TV knows all about "tape-delay" — how what you're seeing or hearing may be seven or more seconds after it actually occurred (so censors can bleep out profanity).

But this performer stacked the deck even further. He was eavesdropping on the station's phone operator, hearing what the person calling in was telling the radio host's screener and staff. He was not just dealing in time-delay, but also "talent-delay."

Oh, by the way, listen and observe the next time you see a performer on television question a "stranger." They may ask the person, "Have we ever met before?" and the person will say no. That doesn't mean something couldn't have been rigged, for a magician can have dozens of assistants, and not all of them actually meet the magician. So when the performer asks "Have we ever met?" the answer "no" may be true ... but that doesn't mean the answerer isn't in the performer's employ.

In addition, there is another clever little ploy that can be used. When a group is involved in a stunt, and the magician asks one of the participants, "Have we ever met?" feel free to wonder why he didn't ask all the other members who were participating.

Talk about staging and misuse of trust! How many times in recent years have we seen a stunt on television in which a group of people surround something as large as an elephant? The camera remains at the level of the people who are standing. It doesn't rise above their heads, but, in order to confine the elephant, all these "volunteers" are surrounding the animal. Even in the back where you cannot see what's going on, you "know" that the animal's confined, and yet, lo and behold, the group opens their circle and the elephant is gone.

What you really need to admire is the acting ability of that group, since when the circle is made and the camera is at the waist level of the crowd, the rear group of people simply open their circle and allow the elephant or person to be lead away. In other words all those people are nothing but faking stooges, and the performer is hoping that no one would think he'd stoop to using dozens of wink-wink collaborators.

You certainly can't credit a performer using such ruses as having the quality, brilliance, and artistry of such truly great magicians as Howard Thurston, Harry Blackstone, or Ricciardi. Google them. They'll never betray your trust.

CHAPTER NINE
THE ADVENTURES OF KRESKIN, ACT ONE

Of the many theories put forth over the years to explain my work, probably the most common has been that my performances are prearranged and that the volunteer subjects are actually paid assistants ("*stooges*" in the language of show business) trained to act out my demonstrations. Perhaps this would make sense were it possible to explain why, after I have spent so many years in the public limelight, not one of the "subjects" has come forward to expose me. Given the enormous sums the tabloid press would be willing to pay for such a fantastic story, any one of literally thousands of subjects would long ago have either publicly cashed in on the conspiracy or privately blackmailed me into bankruptcy were such an outrageous charge even remotely true.

To suggest that the basis for my demonstrations is trickery begs the question and ignores the fact that I have never claimed any supernatural powers or special psychic abilities. As a showman, I naturally reserve the right to embellish my performances with magical touches that heighten the dramatic value of my work without diminishing its legitimacy. I am, after all, an entertainer, not a guinea pig!

When you have made a career of demonstrating unusual abilities, you tend to view similar claims by others with a skeptic's eye, knowing firsthand how difficult it is to achieve such things legitimately. As a case in point, after more than forty years both researching and demonstrating the power of suggestion, I have become absolutely convinced that the so-called state of hypnosis simply does not exist. In other words, there is no special state of mind, condition or trance that can be uniquely characterized as hypnotic.

As I have demonstrated publicly for years, any phenomena that can be produced through suggestion with someone apparently in the hypnotic state can just as readily be produced without a hypnotic state, simply by properly combining persuasion and suggestion with an active and attentive imagination. I'm not saying that people are faking the way they do on many stages in Vegas, pretending to be hypnotized. I'm saying that they're responding legitimately but in a totally conscious state to the power of suggestion that has stimulated their imagination.

If you see such a demonstration in public, it will fall into one of five categories. In the first, the so-called hypnotist works with a group of onstage assistants who are, in fact, plants or stooges, referred to in the fake hypnotic racket as "*horses*," paid actors who travel with the hypnotist and are simply faking their responses. Frankly, such a performance is rarely seen today, although it was quite common in the heyday of vaudeville.

Second, the subjects are legitimate and the hypnotist thinks he is hypnotizing them, but some of them have been trained to respond quickly to his suggestions, being, in fact, preconditioned assistants rather than spontaneous volunteers from the audience. This is a fairly common practice and often these suggestible subjects are paid to travel with the hypnotist's show, much like the "*horses*" of an earlier era.

Third, the hypnotist actually works with total strangers, but whispers instructions to them, cueing them secretly to play along and fake their responses. This is often used by hypnotists who must do a very quick act and, in fact, in France, it is the most common form of stage hypnotism. In the fourth case, the subjects are legitimate, bona fide, untrained volunteers from the audience and the hypnotist leads them through the standard techniques of inducing drowsiness, sleep, etc.

The fifth category is my way of presenting it: a pure demonstration of heightened suggestibility in which legitimate audience volunteers are not subjected to the mumbo-jumbo of hypnotic induction, but nonetheless rapidly behave as though hypnotized in response to persuasion, suggestion and an activated imagination.

There is, in fact, a sixth category of demonstration, which takes things one step beyond what was previously thought possible. In my performances today, I regularly demonstrate my own ability to influence total strangers onstage, causing them to respond to suggestions without even telling them verbally what the suggestions are!

Unfortunately, it is impossible for me to teach this ability—which has taken me years to perfect—within the constraints of a book such as this. And, in fact, even if I *could* communicate this knowledge effectively, there are obvious ethical and legal considerations that would inhibit my doing so.

But I can explain part of my success with this demonstration and how I can consistently achieve positive results so quickly, without resorting to preconditioned volunteers or paid assistants. It is due in part to what some psychologists have termed the "*faith-prestige*" relationship that I have developed and maintain with my audiences. Now let me show you to fake a hypnotic demonstration.

Scene One: Kreskin's Arm Levitation Stunt

Let's assume you have chosen as your subject a young woman named Susan. Have her stand in a doorway facing your group, both her arms hanging at her sides. Now tell her to place her arms against the sides of the door frame, pressing her arms outward, away from her body, as hard as possible, and to continue pressing firmly for thirty to forty-five seconds.

Turn to the audience and say: "In a moment Susan is going to mimic uncontrollably exactly what I do with my arms." Turn back to Susan, telling her to deep pressing firmly outward against sides of the door frame until you reach the count of three. At that time she is to stop pressing, relax her arms and walk forward, away from the doorway.

Count to three and as walks slowly forward, raise both your arms from your sides until they are almost parallel with your shoulders. Amazingly, Susan will seem to respond almost magnetically to your actions, her arms rising by themselves into the air. She will probably be as surprised as your audience.

What is happening here is that the constant outward pressure has produced a muscular condition which can not suddenly be reversed by relaxing that pressure. The muscles involuntarily continue to press outward, as have been conditioned to do, producing the illusion of hypnotic obedience to your suggestion.

Scene Two: Such Nerve

You now announce that you are going to have a friend or it could be even yourself render the strongest man alive unable to lift you or your friend from the floor, despite your or your friend's small frame and light weight. Let's say her name is Lulu. It's someone else other than you are going to be demonstrating it. She will be pressing on a special nerve, you claim, rendering the gentleman powerless to lift her.

First, have the man clasp Lulu around the waist and lift her from the floor, proving his ability to do so without strain under ordinary circumstances. Now have Lulu find the "special nerve" and press on it as he attempts to lift her again. She carefully places her extended forefinger against the man's chin and presses back on it firmly, as you instruct the gentleman to try to the lift again.

Despite every effort, he will be unable to do so. This is because Lulu, by maintaining a firm pressure against his chin, can keep him from bending forward to obtain the necessary leverage. She shouldn't push his head back so far as to make the principle obvious, just enough to keep him slightly off balance.

Scene Three: Paralyzed In A City

Have a subject, preferably a skeptical male, sit in a chair, arms folded, legs outstretched and leaning well back. The small of his back should not be in contact with the back of the chair, but away from it as though he were slouched backward.

Now, in your most impressive voice, "command" him to "relax," as though you were actually "hypnotizing" him. Tell him to lean back and make himself comfortable, keeping his arms folded.

Now this is important: Have him drop his head back so he can look at the ceiling. When he does this, tell him that Lulu is going to find the focal point on his forehead known as the "third eye," used by Eastern mystics to concentrate their attention. Tell him to close his eyes as she presses her index finger against his forehead. Pause dramatically to give the impression of tremendous concentration, then tell him to try to rise from the chair, keeping his arms folded. Tell him he won't be able to do it, no matter how hard he tries, and then tell him to try as hard as he can.

As long as she presses down against his forehead he will find it impossible to stand up. After about ten seconds, say, "All right now, relax. It's all gone, I release you completely." Have Lulu remove her finger from his forehead as you tell him he can rise from the chair now, still keeping his arms folded. In fact, he can and will. If you handle this properly, he will have no idea what really happened.

In fact, what really happened is that Lulu simply kept him off balance! You can prove this to yourself right now as you read my book. Sit in a chair and begin to rise out of it. Notice that the very first thing you must do to get up is to move your head and shoulders forward to bring your center of gravity over your legs.

Now, no matter how much strength you have, you cannot get out of your chair unless and until you move your head forward. But if your head is being held back, the strength of your legs pushing against the floor forces you back into the chair. To move the head forward requires the use of the neck muscles as a whole and Lulu prevented the subject from doing this by pressing down against his forehead, counter acting the use of those muscles.

By having the subject keep his arms folded, you also prevent him from shifting his arm weight forward. So his folded arms and Lulu's index finger pressure conspire (with a little help from Mother Nature!) to pin the subject to his chair. If you stage this dramatically, using the commanding voice quality of the stage hypnotist, you will create the convincing illusion of having influenced the subject to respond to your "hypnotic" suggestion.

Scene Four: The Spirit Touch

This stunt is best done alone with a single subject. If others are watching, it becomes too much of a joke at the subject's expense. Let's assume your subject for this is a woman. Ask her to sit in a chair that is backed against a wall. You claim this is to make certain there is no one behind her, but in fact it is to prevent her from pulling back her head and opening her eyes prematurely should she become startled. You do not want that to happen, as it will expose your trickery.

Instruct her to close her eyes, telling her that you will then lightly place your right forefinger against her left eyelid and your left forefinger lightly against her right eyelid. With your fingers in contact with her eyelids, you will call upon a spirit from the past, asking it to give a sign of its presence. Emphasize to her that she must keep her eyes tightly shut until you withdraw your fingers. Point out that closing the eyes simulates the total darkness of a traditional séance.

Almost as soon as her eyes are closed, she will feel a slight tap on her arm or neck. Remove your fingers from her eyelids, holding them an inch or two away and ask her to open her eyes. She does, and you innocently ask if she felt anything. Of course, she did, so you propose to try to take it a step further.

Ask her to close her eyes again, and again place your forefingers in contact with her closed eyelids.

This time she'll feel a slight cold breeze on the side of her neck. Remove your fingers and ask for her report. You then propose one final attempt. She closes her eyes again and you place your forefingers gently against her eyelids. This time she'll feel something passing through her hair and may be so startled that she tries to open her eyes, in spite of your earlier admonitions and the contact of your forefingers. Prepare to be amazed yourself when you hear her describe her spirit experience to others!

The secret of this stunt is ingeniously simple. When the subject closes her eyes the first time, don't touch the eyelids with the two forefingers, but with the forefinger and middle finger of a single hand, one finger on each eyelid. It will feel to her just as though you were pressing both forefingers against her eyelids, as you claimed, but in fact one hand is entirely free and you use it to touch her very lightly and quickly on the neck or shoulder.

Immediately bring your free hand back in front of her eyes, forefinger extended, and simultaneously remove the other fingers from the eyes, curling your middle finger into the palm. Thus, when she opens her eyes, she sees both hands in position, forefingers extended. You ask what happened, and if your secret touch was sufficiently subtle you may be surprised by her response. This helps create greater anticipation and the feeling that something very ethereal is taking place.

Scene Five: The Imaginary Insect

The secret here is a four- or five-inch piece of stiff black horsehair attached to one of your fingernails. If horses are scarce in your neighborhood, the black synthetic thread used to stiffen sport coats may also be used. Using a small piece of tape, attach the hair or thread to the back of your forefinger so that it extends straight out from the finger. The hair or thread may be longer if its stiffness is sufficient to prevent it from dangling down when the finger points horizontally.

If you pay no attention to your hands, neither will anyone else, and the hair will pass unnoticed.

Let's assume your subject is a gentleman. When the time for this demonstration arrives, have him close his eyes. Set the stage by suggesting that he is going to feel something moving along the right side of his face, and as you do this, make gestures close to his face with both hands, taking care not to touch him with your hands, but allowing the hair occasionally to brush across the skin on the right side of his face. He will sense this immediately, but with his eyes closed will not be able to discern its true nature.

When he reports the sensation, keep suggesting that a bug is flying around, brushing against his face and crawling into his ear. As you make the latter suggestion, the hair should be passing over his ear. Keep your hands in motion and allow the hair to touch the inside of his ear. This will be quite irritating, and when the subject begins to move his hand upward to scratch or slap the bug, move your hands away as you clap them together and tell him the bug is gone, the suggestion is lifted. To your friends, it will look as though you have brought to a dramatic conclusion a Kreskin test of suggestibility.

Scene Six: Checkmate

As a case in point, consider my blindfold chess challenge of Karpov and Korchnoi a few years back. As you may recall, Karpov and Korchnoi were bitter chess rivals vying for the world championship title. It was a classic confrontation: Korchnoi, the Soviet defector, versus Karpov, the Soviet champion. Much of the media attention became focused on Korchnoi's accusation that the Soviets were using a hypnotist to break his concentration. And, in fact, the Soviets did place a prominent Russian hypnotist in the front row of the tournament audience.

This was, of course, a classic example of one-upmanship, designed to throw Korchnoi off balance, which it did most effectively. Years earlier Jimmy Grippo, the legendary magician, card manipulator and hypnotist, was similarly retained by several prizefighters to "psyche out" their opponents. He would stand at ringside, staring intensely at the other fighter, supposedly "zapping" him with "hypnotic powers."

In any case, I decided to challenge both Korchnoi and Karpov when their tournament was over. I would play both of them simultaneously and blindfolded to boot! A prominent Olympic chess coach who had helped train Bobby Fischer announced publicly that I was just talking through my hat and that if I did go through with it, he would eat his!

To everyone's surprise, both Korchnoi and Karpov accepted my challenge and agreed to the tournament. Unfortunately, Karpov had already returned to the Soviet Union and was unable to obtain a travel visa to return to New York, while Korchnoi, the defector, clearly could not go to Moscow. Fortunately, the chess columnist for *The New York Times* agreed to stand in for Karpov, confident of his proven ability to play a half dozen or more games simultaneously.

Now picture me, sitting in the United Nations Plaza Hotel with an audience that included some of the world's most famous chess officials and television crews from around the world, and I was supposed to take on two of the world's leading chess experts while blindfolded! An eye surgeon was brought in to provide the blindfold. She had devised and tested a method of blindfolding herself securely, and she applied this same blindfolding method to me.

Now let me point out that I did not expect to win both games under these conditions. Having only played chess a half dozen times in my life, I was simply hoping to hold my own for a respectable period of time. In fact, I found out later that Korchnoi had wagered that the contest would be over in under ten minutes. More than an hour later, I was still playing both men, although all I could do was announce my moves, being unable to see either board.

Ultimately, I announced a move and lost to Korchnoi. At that moment he jumped up and ran to the back of the room, announcing that he knew how I had done it. He spoke with Mark Finston, a fine feature writer for the *Newark Star Ledger* in New Jersey, telling him, "Kreskin is reading my thoughts, because I keep thinking. I wrote a note to you saying that if Kreskin castled at this point, he would lose the game, and that's just what happened."

Of course, Korchnoi was right. Chess players constantly analyze the board, thinking several moves ahead, anticipating their opponents' best moves. By taking advantage of this, I was able to get the players to play against themselves, until Korchnoi deliberately concentrated on a losing move for me! Incidentally, though I never did have the pleasure of seeing Bobby Fischer's coach eat his hat and though I did not win either game, the one against the chess columnist for the *New York Times* ran nearly two hours!

Scene Seven: Blindfold Basics

Sometimes in my concert performances, I will be blindfolded and have a balloon tossed into the audience where it gets bounced among the thousands of spectators until finally it comes to rest at a random location. With a subject walking close behind me concentrating on the location of the balloon, I will make my way blindfolded through the audience until I finally break the balloon with a needle. Let me show you two methods for simulating such a test through trickery.

Simply take a handkerchief and fold it into a thick, opaque bundle which you tie behind your head so that it covers your eyes. The thickness of the handkerchief will prevent you from looking straight ahead, but if you look down, you'll be able to see the floor through the gaps between the handkerchief and the sides of your nose. This is the traditional "magician's peek".

Here's how you can use these methods to convince your friends of your Kreskin-like abilities: Leave the room and have one of your friends hide among the others. While this is happening, you are being blindfolded outside the room. When you are led back inside, you pretend to pick up on the thoughts of the audience, leading you to your friend, whom you tap on the shoulder.

Obviously, this will present no difficulty if you can see straight ahead, as in the first method. But what if your sight is limited to the downward peek? Tipping your head back would make it obvious that you are peeking along your nose. The secret is to make a mental note of the kind of shoe your friend is wearing. Then, as you walk through the group, look for the shoes, and tap your friend on the shoulder. You will stun your audience.

CHAPTER TEN

THE ADVENTURES OF KRESKIN, ACT TWO

Scene Eight: A Legitimate Telepathic Test

When I was about nine years old I began to practice magic tricks. Magic became an obsessive interest and its practice became the focal point of my extracurricular activities, a condition persisting through my teenage years. But even before reaching my teens, I had begun to find that I could accomplish by legitimate means many of the tricks I was working so hard to learn to fake. In other words, I was using genuine abilities to simulate fake ones! With this realization was born my ambition to become a legitimate mentalist.

The following test marked a turning point in my life. For many years I would not discuss it, but I can clearly remember repeating the test time and again for relatives, teachers, classmates and neighbors when I was only nine or ten years old and getting *true results*!

Now you may be wondering why I am including a legitimate test here, since the purpose of these chapters is not to teach you to become a genuine telepathist or mentalist, but rather to fake what I do in my public performances. Well, for decades people have reported that while faking paranormal activity, they have actually begun to experience genuine phenomena which they could not explain. Naturally, there are those who would like to believe that those people are merely deceiving themselves, but having had this experience myself, I am convinced otherwise and urge you to give this a try. And as your reward, I'll show you afterward how you can simulate it by trickery!

One other person is required for the test and it is best if this is someone with whom you feel a close rapport. Take six to eight cards from a deck and lay them in a random order face up in a row on the table, spaced about two inches apart. This test can, in fact, be done with the cards facedown, but you will find it easier at the beginning to work with the cards face up, giving the sender you are working with a clear visual focus on which to concentrate. Ask the other person to think of one of the cards and to let you know when he or she is ready to proceed.

Now, your mood is critically important. Try not to think of anything at all and, in particular, do not try to guess the card on which the sender is concentrating. Hold your hand about three inches above the outer edge of the first card in the row. You can hold it higher, if this is more comfortable, the important thing being that it begins over the first card. You then proceed to move it slowly along the entire row, passing over each card until you have reached the outer edge of the last card in the row.

After a brief pause, reverse the procedure, passing your hand over the cards in the opposite direction. Go back and forth several times.

As you continue this process, you will notice that your hand seems to dip over some portion of the row. Don't try to analyze this tendency or rationalize it and especially take care not to exaggerate it. Just let it happen. Countless studies have shown that intellectual reasoning, critical analysis, and conscious skepticism all inhibit telepathic communication. Gradually slow the motion of your hand until you clearly recognize over which card it is dipping. Once you are certain of the card, pick it up and ask your subject if it is the one on which he or she is concentrating. If you are using six cards, your chances of being correct purely by chance are only one in six. If, however, you are beginning to become sensitized to the inclinations of your subject, you will find your success rate will be much, much higher.

Don't be discouraged if you are not successful at first, and don't expect one hundred percent accuracy with every sender with whom you work. Even after many years' experience with this test, I would never expect or claim an accuracy rate of one hundred percent. Incidentally, if your first choice is wrong, ask your subject to concentrate on the card again, actually trying to visualize it, but keeping both eyes open and watching you as you move your hand. You may also wish to try closing you eyes and ask someone else to observe your hand, watching for the slight dipping over a particular card. If you succeed even one-third of the time, you will still be well ahead of the law of averages. As you begin this experiment, you will probably find that when you pick the wrong card, it will be just beside the right one.

If your initial success rate is no better than dictated by chance, there may be several things going on that are worth examining. First, telepathic communication is largely an unconscious activity and you may be overwhelming it with conscious processes. You might also be trying too hard, introducing a tension into the procedure that interferes with your sensitivity.

Under stress, you may actually be responding to an autosuggestion regarding the choice—in effect reading your own mind, rather than that of your sender. Finally, if your success rate is well below what even chance would dictate, then you may, in fact, be responding to the sender but consistently misinterpreting the signals. Often this can be remedied by simply making the opposite choices in subsequent tests, countering your intuition to correct its bias.

Scene Nine: One in a Million

You'll need a writing pad with fairly small sheets and a bowl. Instead of having your friends jot down a thought, ask each of them to call out a three-digit number. You repeat the number and write it down on a slip of paper, which you then fold twice and drop into the bowl. This is repeated for each number called out, with all the pieces folded identically so you cannot be accused of marking the slips to keep track of them. When each person has named a number (and with a small group, you can have each person name several numbers, going around the group more than once), hand someone the bowl and ask him or her to mix up the slips and then pick one out of the bowl. Take back the bowl, walk away and ask the spectator with the slip to open it up and silently read the number on the paper, without revealing it to anyone else. After concentrating for a moment, you pause dramatically and then announce a number, which proves to be the one the spectator was thinking of, as can be verified by passing the slip of paper around the group.

Unless you have developed the abilities that I demonstrate throughout the world, you will need to cheat for this test to succeed every time. Here's' how you do it: Let's say the first number called out is 351. Repeat it, write it down, fold up the paper and drop it into the bowl. No matter what numbers are called out, repeat them aloud, but always write the first number, 351, on the skips. Ultimately, you will have a bowl filled with identical folded slips each bearing the number 351!

Once the spectator has mixed the slips and removed one of them from the bowl, take back the bowl and move away from the spectator. Apparently you are doing this to avoid seeing the number on the chosen slip, but really you are getting the bowl (with its incriminating evidence!) away from the center of attention. After you have revealed the number, you can keep the heat off the bowl by focusing attention on the slip of paper that is being passed around. Don't sell this stunt short. If you take it seriously and keep your cool, your friends will credit you with Kreskin-like powers!

Scene Ten: Kreskin's Mass Audience Projection

In most of my concerts I demonstrate the ability to influence a mass audience by attempting the mental projection of a single thought – be it a name, number, scene or feeling – to everyone attending my program. On occasion, as many as six and even seven thousand people have succeeded in picking up the very thought that I was projecting. Let me show you a way to simulate the Kreskin Mass Audience Projection Test, creating the illusion that you have duplicated my feat. If you have a group of friends together at a table or in a room, they'll get quite a kick out of this.

Give everyone a pad of paper and a pencil and tell them to write down a three-digit number, with all the digits different, taking care not to show the number to anyone. Now tell them to reverse the order of the digits, creating another three-digit number. Instruct them to subtract the smaller of the two numbers from the larger. For example, 471 reversed yields 174, which is then to be subtracted from 471, yielding in this example 297 (471-174=297). The digits of the total are to be similarly reversed and then added to the original total. In our example, 297 plus 792 yields 1,089. When audience members have arrived at a total, ask those having a four-digit number to raise their hands. All those who do will also have arrived at 1,089, apparently demonstrating your ability at mass projection, while in fact demonstrating the consistency of mathematics!

Scene Eleven:
The Kreskin Compulsion Experiment

On another page is a diagram resembling a checkerboard. It consists of sixteen "windows," eight are circles and eight are squares. Inside each window is the name of a celebrity. You may wish to make a larger version of this pattern for your demonstrations, perhaps even drawing it on a chalkboard, and you may substitute your name for mine and those of your friends for those of the other celebrities. When you are ready to begin, point out to the participants that they will be able to move in straight lines, either up and down vertically, side to side horizontally, or diagonally. Of course, they cannot move outside the borders of the board. You should memorize the following instructions so you'll be able to give them with your back to the board. That should be easy, as there are only five moves. In fact, try them now so you'll experience the effect.

First, place your finger on any name that is in a square. You can look for a favorite, or choose one at random. Now move your finger left or right to the nearest circle. Next move up or down to the nearest square. Now move diagonally to the nearest circle. Finally, move either right or down to the nearest square. Incredibly, you will have arrived at the one square bearing the name "Kreskin"!

If you do this for a group, with each participant following along on his or her own board, the effect is positively eerie. On my television series, which was syndicated worldwide, I performed this for Bill Shatner of *Star Trek* fame as a demonstration of how paranormal phenomena could be faked. He found it most intriguing, but I have often wondered how his television counterpart Mr. Spock would have reacted! "Eminently logical," would probably have been his response, because the structure actually demands that anyone who follows my directions will end up on the Kreskin square. This stunt has been done many, many times by a variety of magicians in magic specials. Now you can see that it works mechanically, but wait until you get to see the response of the person or persons you're doing this with.

Scene Twelve: Color Divination

Occasionally over the years, rather than have subjects think of a name, a series of digits or even a picture, I have asked them to paint a color in their minds or picture a scene in which a single color predominates. This is an interesting exercise and a departure from the more traditional thought-reading experiments.

I am going to show you a diabolical way to create the illusion that you can perceive a color being thought of by your subject. Try this. It will stun your participant. You'll need a small, opaque paper bag and a box of crayons, the more colors in the box the better. Hold both the open crayon box and the open paper bag behind your back, one in each hand. Ask your subject to take the crayon box, select and remove one crayon from it, hand you the crayon and then close up the box, all of this done behind your back.

When you are handed the crayon, you immediately drop it into the bag, which you then crumple up and hand to your subject for safekeeping. The assisting spectator now holds both the closed crayon box and the crumpled bag containing the chosen crayon. Point out that both are closed and opaque, offering no clue as to the contents. Ask the spectator to hold the paper bag up to the light, pointing out that no one can see the contents. Ask the spectator to shake the bag, pointing out that this also gives no clue as to the color of the crayon. Now place both your hands around the bag and crush it further, as though you were sensing the color through the bag. You now announce a color, stating, for example, that the crayon is purple. Your subject will admit with surprise that this is the chosen color, and you then dramatically rip open the bag to extract the crayon, which you display triumphantly.

Of course, there is no real telepathy involved in this stunt, which merely imitates one of my demonstrations. The secret is well hidden as it takes place behind your back. When the spectator assisting you hands you the crayon, you ask him or her to close the crayon box. While the spectator is briefly occupied with this, drop the chosen crayon into the bag, but in the process nick one of the ends of the crayon with a thumbnail, leaving a big of its color under your nail. You immediately close the bag and hand it to the spectator. When you later place your hands around the bag to crush it further, a quick glance at your thumbnail will tell you all you need to know.

Scene Thirteen: Teleportation

I am sharing with you some of the fakery utilized in apparent psychic demonstrations. Don't shortchange what you're about to read. It turned out that when this was first done, it fooled a whole group of magicians.

The following stunt was a favorite of the great Houdini. We are told that he liked to do this for private gatherings at his home, at banquets, and even at meetings of the Society of American Magicians, over which he presided for many years prior to his death in 1926. You'll be able to do this with people standing all around you, carefully watching every move. Take out an old coin or some other intriguing small object about which you can weave an interesting story, such as a rusty key from a haunted house, a good luck talisman from an Indian Yogi or a Gypsy's finger ring. Introduce the object and openly place it on the palm of your left hand.

Take an opaque handkerchief with your right hand and carefully cover the left hand, pointing out that you will not touch the hand as you cover it. This, you explain, is because everyone knows that there are swift and secret means of stealing such an object by sleight of hand and you want everyone to be absolutely certain at this point that it is still on the left palm, even though they can't see it.

Often someone will express doubt concerning the object's whereabouts at this point, which is perfect for your purposes. Ask that person to reach under the handkerchief and verify by touch that the object is still there. Should no one express such doubts, simply ask someone to reach under the handkerchief to feel the object. They will testify that the object is still on the left palm. Ask another person to repeat this action, then another, and another until there truly can be no doubt regarding the existence and location of the object. At that point, draw attention to your right hand by snapping its fingers over the handkerchief.

Announce that the coin has been mysteriously teleported and then grab one corner of the handkerchief with the right hand and instantly pull it off the left hand. The coin has vanished without a trace. Magicians are often accused of using their sleeves to accomplish their tricks, but this can be done with the sleeves rolled up. In fact, you could feature this at a nudist colony! Later, as people mill around, someone will suddenly spot the ring on the side of a chair or on a shelf, having apparently been paranormally teleported to that location.

This mysterious feat is accomplished through the subtle use of a secret assistant. You need only make sure that your accomplice is the last person to feel the object under the handkerchief. Not only does he or she feel it, but actually steals it away in a loosely closed hand while verbally confirming its presence on your palm! You then place some distance between yourself and your accomplice as you talk about the mysterious event about to transpire.

This gives your assistant a chance to set the object down casually where it will be discovered later. Once you whisk away the handkerchief, everyone will begin looking around to see where it might have gone. You'll be surprised by their reaction when they spontaneously find it, another example of the powerful force of the human imagination, focused in this case on the theme of teleportation.

Scene Fourteen: The Sniff Test

Explain how my check is hidden at each of my performances and that I proceed to locate it by thought perception. Explain that you will attempt a Kreskin-like test. When you leave the room, you explain, a committee is to single out one person in the entire room. When you return to the room, everyone is to sit or stand still, without speaking.

You then leave the room, escorted by one or two others who verify that you do not eavesdrop on the room in your absence. When you return, begin to walk quietly around the room. This may be a gathering of ten or fifteen friends, a classroom of thirty or forty, or perhaps even a congregation at a festival with seventy or more present. As you quietly walk through the gathering, suddenly place your hands on someone's shoulder and announce that this is the chosen one. You will be right.

Here is the secret for faking this stunt: You do have a confederate in the audience, a secret assistant, but he does not have any fancy electronic devices to communicate with you. When you ask your audience to become totally silent so that you can concentrate, everyone will turn to watch your progress. As you pass near the chosen person, your secret assistant simply sniffles once or twice.

Because of the silence, and because you are listening for it, you will have no trouble picking up this signal. As you focus your attention on specific individuals in that area, your assistant again sniffles discreetly as you approach the chosen person. A sniffle is an entirely natural part of the background noise and will pass completely unnoticed by those not listening for it, though it will be obvious to you.

While you may not have met the Kreskin challenge by using thought transference or telepathy, you can take some pride in the fact that with just a few sniffles you have duplicated what other fake

Kreskins needed thousands of dollars of electronics to achieve!

ADDENDUM

B(U)Y THE BOOK

Years ago as a young man, I met a performer who had fled Switzerland during the rise of Nazism and had come to the United States. While he was only fairly successful in the western world, he was a brilliant performer. His name was Dr. Jaks ... Stanley Jaks. The real beauty of his performance was in his climactic stunt — which I need to tell you he did legitimately. In this case, there was no trickery. It was for real, which made it all the more thrilling.

He would have on the table an easel that only went up to about waist level in front of him. He would have himself blindfolded, then someone would come forward and write their name using taking a thick, felt-like, pencil. They would then hand Dr. Jaks the pen. In a matter of seconds, with the pen in his hand, still blindfolded, he wrote above it, upside down, an exact duplicate of the name the person wrote — and in the same style of writing. He had forged their penmanship and successfully written it upside down. Even if he could somehow see what they had written through the blindfold, it was still most startling that he could recreate it upside down. It was a brilliant piece of artistic skill and showmanship.

I met Dr. Jaks when he was sitting with a conjuring publisher who would later become his friend. To a degree, Jaks was lonely man since he was not achieving the same fame in the U.S. that he had in Europe. He shook hands with me and, in shaking his hand, I felt his loneliness, but also his honesty. Years later, when Dr. Jaks passed away, I received an unexpected message. His attorney, who was very close to him, came to me and said the feeling was that I should have Jaks' books.

I was impressed to discover that, through years of travels, he had obtained manuscripts that dealt with the trickery and deceptions used by psychics, psychic acts, psychic performers, and the rest. Some were very, very private, some were sent to him by the "psychics" themselves, and some were acquired in rare, out-of-the-way curiosity shops. Every few years, the good doctor would go to a book-binder and have these papers secured into a hard bound volume. Talk about a rare piece of priceless research!

When he died, there were fifty-four volumes — all the size of textbooks. I was quite overwhelmed, and felt a great inner joy to have such literally priceless material. I accepted the books gratefully and, dare I say, even humbly. Even so, I discovered there was only one book missing. That book contained the manuscripts of the magical effects that Dr. Jaks created himself. That volume went to a member of his family, which I certainly didn't begrudge. Besides, I already had copies of all his writings and the descriptions of his creations.

Dr. Jaks' library — those remarkable books — is in a special place amongst my memorabilia, and I decided some years ago to find out just how priceless they would be to the magical community. Besides you, dear reader, there's probably only two-dozen people who know what the largest offer was for these volumes. It is more than anything ever recorded in conjuring literature. For I can tell you, as the gentleman who represented me when we looked into the possibility of offering these books for sale, that the last bid was $1,250,000 … but with a final bidder saying he would pay ten percent over any final price. We were not told who the bidder was, but his rep revealed it was a very famous American stage illusionist of the 1980's and 90's.

I intend to put these volumes up for sale eventually. The books will never be turned over to a library, since I found out years ago how Houdini's books have been treated by The Library of Congress. I was told by reputable sources that when they were escorted to see the books in person, they were shocked to find out that they were largely in the exact same boxes that they had been in when they were first delivered after Houdini's death. They had never even been filed properly.

Since then I have learned that priceless volumes on science, medicine, philosophy, and many other important subjects have been damaged and even have disappeared. Clearly, the reverence and protection of such a library as Dr. Jaks' will not be one of a public library — not any more. Something has changed in modern culture. So if the books are not bought by someone who will value them for what they are truly worth, I have another plan. I will burn them.

Before anyone comes forward and says how dare you do such a thing, know this. Knowledge is important, even sacred, I totally agree. But some knowledge is never meant to be spread irresponsibly. Certainly not knowledge that a man like Dr. Jaks valued with such care, and protected between hand-binded, hard-bound covers.

As of this writing, the Jaks writings are for sale, and whatever the bids, nothing under four million dollars will be accepted. And if the volumes are not purchased and protected, I consider it a much greater honor to Dr. Jaks to have his books destroyed.

AFTERWORD

If there's a further truth I would want to share with you, dear reader, it is the fact that I look upon my career as an adventure. Year after year I've taken on new challenges, and I've also found around me activities and developments that only add more impact and import to my work. Despite an incredibly hectic schedule, I've been told by more than one national network newsman that there's probably greater interest and need for my kind of entertainment than ever before. How true: it has touched audiences all over the western world. And I suspect the same would hold true when I travel out of this part of our earthly environment.

Oh, by the way, don't ever get the impression that I only believe in telepathy and thought transference.

There are phenomena that I think is worthy of greater investigation — including other areas of paranormal activity. Even the field of UFO's deserves a vast range of interest and research ... although I don't really think anyone has visited this earth. If they do, I'm not really sure they'd want to spend too much time here, considering the way mankind is behaving at the present.

So do not label me a skeptic. First, I can't stand labels. Second, I am skeptical about some things, but most skeptics are nothing more than cynics, locked like a post-hypnotic suggestion into one way of thinking. In my childhood, I came to believe that much of what was done by trickery could be done legitimately. It was because of one of the most important tools of my life ... imagination.

It's also one that I fear is being threatened today. Threatened by the plethora of cell phones, the internet, and all kinds of "picture boxes." It's threatened by our just sitting in front of something, rather than moving, sharing personal activities with others, and sparking one's mind even further. In short, the imagination is being threatened by its lack of use.

I'm seeing it more in youngsters, as teachers in grade school point out to me that they see a lessening in their students' imaginations. They don't go out and play together very much any more. They don't create their own group activities. They have electronic machines and all kinds of junk to do that for them. If this continues unabated, we risk losing one of man's greatest tools — the tool that made individuals rise against adversity, whether it was war, famine, weather, finances, or family problems.

It is the tool that we dare not endanger. It is the tool that can solve every problem, overcome every obstacle, and set any goal. It is our "imagination."

Appropriate to the above, let it be known that I have for years offered $50,000 to anyone who can prove that I employ confederates in any phase of my program, and that remains such as of today. But there is one more additional factor I have decided to add to reinforce the credibility and legitimacy of what I do. The additional factor has been inspired by the release of *The Great Buck Howard*.

It simply is this. I will also now offer, for the rest of my career, the sum of one million dollars to anybody who can prove that I use secret hidden electronic devices to aid in the accomplishment of my telepathic tests.

In that spirit, and with apologies to David Letterman, here is my own "Top Ten List." Tonight's subject: "The Top Ten Ways Critics Think Kreskin Does What He Does (all of which have been theorized but never justified or proven).

Number ten: Kreskin's mother spies on the audience with binoculars from the rafters and transmits the information to him on a miniature radio receiver hidden in his eyeglass frames.

Number nine: Kreskin achieves X-ray vision by shining a special intense light on the audience to render packages and envelopes transparent.

Number eight: Kreskin hires a private eye to dig up dirt on his audience before each show.

Number seven: The pads and pencils Kreskin gives the audience to use have radar systems imbedded in them.

Number six: Kreskin forces audience members to write their innermost thoughts on a special pad with carbon paper hidden inside.

Number five: Kreskin can make anyone say anything anytime through the power of suggestion.

Number four: Kreskin steals information when no one is looking.

Number three: It's all done with stooges.

Number two: Kreskin is just a darn good guesser.

And the *number one* way critics think Kreskin does what he does: Kreskin is the luckiest man alive!

Between you and me, my friends, the last one, number one, is true. But only because of your interest, support, and kindness over the years. For that, I sincerely give thanks. Because of all of you, I am, indeed, the luckiest man alive.

And, with that, I'm not going to say farewell, dear reader ... simply "to be continued."

LaVergne, TN USA
28 December 2009
168296LV00001B/119/P